PRAISE FOR THE AUTHOR

It is a happy event to go on a course for one day and find that it's neither time nor money wasted. For any person who gets interviewed or 'asked for comment' by the media, I highly recommend Pete's training. The chance of future media embarrassment or anxiety has now been dramatically reduced, made possible by the pragmatic tutoring and the emphasis on practice in order to learn. This is not one of those theory courses where only a small proportion is relevant, this one is full on from the get go and the day goes by quickly. Well worth it.

Josie Ogden (CEO)

I found the strategies suggested in our session with Pete Burdon very useful in thinking through how best to phrase media responses and be assured of getting our intended message reported. Rather than being bogged down in theory, the use of practical exercises made this course both pragmatically applicable and hugely enjoyable – and you can't say that about most day-long courses!

Mike Brown (CEO)

Recently I was fortunate enough to have a fascinating training day with Pete Burdon. The whole day was sensational and I cannot recommend enough that all owners and/or managers of retirement villages and residential care facilities, should attend. I think it is essential. In our industry we never know when a public relations issue can occur and Pete gives simple and clear tools to deal with those moments. I cannot recommend enough that you attend this course.

Graham Wilkinson (Company Director)

Pete's workshop presented a comprehensive and practical set of skills and strategies on communicating key messages to the media that I used immediately on my return to my workplace. Pete's knowledge from both a journalism and public relations perspective gave me invaluable insights on how best to create relevant, clear messages and how to deliver them authentically to the media. Highly recommended and many thanks to Pete.

Sharon O'Laughlin (Communication Manager)

Without Pete's training I would have most likely ended up on the "front page" for the wrong reason! This workshop was focused, real and practical and provided me with the opportunity to learn the skills to confidently front the media and remain in total control. In film or in print, we cannot afford our comments or messages to miss the mark. This training is essential for any leader who needs to communicate with clarity, confidence and under pressure. It's professional insurance that you cannot afford to be without!

Rob Callaghan (School Principal)

Often, saying 'no comment' and rejecting the media outright is not a good thing for your client. After Pete's training, I have the tools to see that my clients get the best kind of media coverage when I'm involved.

Andrew Logie (Law Firm Partner)

A challenging, interesting and rewarding day. Through classroom based discussion, advice and lots of very practical exercises I now feel equipped to plan and manage that critical media interaction that may be just around the next corner. Pete's industry knowledge and insights are invaluable.

Jonathan Cross (Board Chairperson)

Staff who attended the training with Pete Burdon have reported an increased knowledge base and development of skills required to deal effectively with the media. The presenter's subject matter expertise was excellent. The session was very practical and those in attendance had a number of opportunities to be interviewed on camera and received relevant feedback.

Doctor Julia Peters (Professional and Clinical Director)

I found the training really helpful and took away some key learnings that I'll use the next time I'm confronted with an interview situation. The way Pete set up interview scenarios, recorded them and played them back for the participants to see and comment on was a really powerful way for us to understand the points he was making.

Jimmy Tupou (Professional Rugby Player)

Pete is an expert at getting good publicity. When in government I remember weeks when I got more media coverage than the Prime Minister and Pete was a major factor in making that possible.

Maurice Williamson (Former Cabinet Minister)

I attended Pete Burdon's 'Introduction to Becoming an Effective Media Spokesperson' session at the PRINZ Conference in 2014 and learnt lots, despite having run my own media training sessions with clients. Pete was well-prepared, engaging and provided us with some hands-on, practical ways to become better spokespeople. I'd endorse his services not only for those wanting to become better in this field but also for those PR practitioners advising clients, CEOs and executives on conducting media interviews.

Bruce Fraser (Public Relations Institute of New Zealand (PRINZ) President 2014-2016)

MEDIA
TRAINING
FOR MODERN LEADERS

GLOBAL
PUBLISHING
G R O U P

Global Publishing Group
Australia • New Zealand • Singapore • America • London

MEDIA TRAINING
FOR MODERN LEADERS

How to face the news media with
confidence in today's world

PETE BURDON

First Edition 2015

National Library of Australia
Cataloguing-in-Publication entry:

Creator: Burdon, Peter R. (Peter Rowland), 1970- author.

Media Training For Modern Leaders: How to Face the News Media with Confidence in Today's World / Pete Burdon.

1st ed.
ISBN: 9781925288025 (paperback)

Public relations personnel – Training of.
Press secretaries – Training of.
Communication in politics.
Public relations and politics.
Public speaking.

Dewey Number: 352.232748

Published by Global Publishing Group
PO Box 517 Mt Evelyn, Victoria 3796 Australia
Email info@GlobalPublishingGroup.com.au

For further information about orders:
Phone: +61 3 9739 4686 or Fax +61 3 8648 6871

I dedicate this book to five very special people. Firstly, my late father, John Burdon, who never had the opportunities I've had. John had many gifts including an amazing grasp of the English language but circumstances meant he was never in a position to unleash them.

I must thank my mother, Be Burdon. She's done so much for me throughout my life. What stands out most is her total confidence in me. Her belief in me helped me maintain belief in myself.

I could never write a book without thanking my wife Stephanie and daughter Olivia. My life has been incredibly enriched since they came into it. Their love and support is what has made this book possible.

Finally, my sister Julia deserves a mention. She's always been there for me. She's a great friend and someone I can always count on.

Pete Burdon

ACKNOWLEDGEMENTS

To everyone at Global Publishing, thanks for all you've done. Darren's knowledge of the publishing industry is second to none while his marketing advice is priceless. I've never met someone so talented and yet so incredibly modest at the same time. Kelly also deserves a special mention for the tireless work she puts in for her authors.

I couldn't write a media training book without acknowledging a special chief reporter I worked under as a journalist. Hugh O'Donnell was taken from this life far too soon. One piece of his advice that has always stuck with me is, "Every time you can say something with one word instead of two, it's like winning five dollars."

I must acknowledge another special reporter I worked with. When I began my career as a journalist in a small town where I didn't know a soul, Pete Franklin took me under his wing. He showed me the ropes, acted as a great sounding board and became a good friend.

I also thank former Cabinet Minister, Maurice Williamson, and his Senior Private Secretary, Bride Wilkinson, for taking me on as Press Secretary all those years ago. They gave me my start in political media relations at a relatively young age which stood me in great stead for my future career. I can't thank them enough.

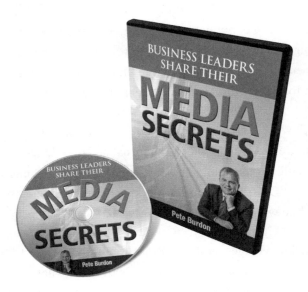

CONTENTS

FOREWORD

Leaders and communicators need to understand the news media and how it affects reputation. Media savvy leaders embrace the opportunity and see the media as a chance to protect or grow their reputation. Those who don't understand the media may suffer when a negative issue takes place. They don't know how to respond, can panic and often suffer reputational damage as a consequence.

Pete outlines what the modern leader needs to know about the news media. A large part of this is how to master media interviews. In a clear and practical style, his book covers traditional media training principles and new ones that have emerged in digital media such as how to prepare for a Skype interview.

Pete covers other aspects of the news media in the book including communicating in a crisis and how to generate positive media attention, making the book ideal for a public relations professional and anyone in a leadership role. It's a comprehensive resource that explains how to deal with the news media in any scenario.

Pete is an active member of PRINZ, having presented at a national conference and conducted workshops for members.

On a personal note, I took part in one of Pete's workshops, which was beneficial in preparing me for media interviews at the time.

'*Media Training for Modern Leaders*' covers techniques that are valuable in building your confidence and getting important points through to your audience.

Simone Bell
(CEO, Public Relations Institute of New Zealand) (PRINZ)

INTRODUCTION

The ability to face the news media with confidence has never been more important than it is for today's leaders. Many of the pressures are the same as they were 30 years ago but some have changed.

Leaders from all walks of life must be ready for that unexpected media interview. That's nothing new. Fear of humiliation at the hands of a television presenter has been around since the advent of television news. Concern at the possibility of being taken out of context or misquoted by a press reporter is also as old as the newspaper itself.

It's a well-known fact that newspaper circulation numbers have been dwindling throughout the world as more people access online sites for their news. What's less well known is that news is often posted on these sites almost as soon as it happens. That means media spokespeople need to be ready to talk almost immediately in many situations. The alternative is a brief sentence at the end of the story: "Mr Blogs refused to comment."

This need for speed wasn't important before the digital age. In those days, people either got their news from the evening television bulletin or tomorrow's newspaper. That meant there was less urgency for reporters to get their stories out immediately.

The changing role of journalists also changes how modern leaders must approach media interviews. There are fewer specialist reporters working in newsrooms now and a new job title is becoming more widespread across the world. The multimedia journalist is someone who produces news in different formats for the same organisation. That may include a written story for the traditional newspaper before following up with a video alternative for the website. As these roles grow, spokespeople must come to terms with multi-modal interview formats.

Reporters are also social media experts. Not only do they use Facebook, Twitter and many other platforms to source their news, they continually post stories on these sites. This allows bad news to spread like wildfire, multiplying the damage for anyone who's misquoted or taken out of context.

Another area is equally as critical. The demands of communicating effectively in a crisis have grown significantly in the digital age. As a modern leader, it's important that you understand these changes and what's needed to make sure your organisation is ready. While you may have public relations staff to manage this, you still need to know what to do and what role you must play when things go wrong.

About the book

The book focuses on everything the modern leader must know when it comes to media relations in the digital age. That makes it a valuable resource for the novice leader and spokesperson as well as the seasoned campaigner.

The process of becoming an effective media spokesperson is the same as becoming an expert in any field. Just ask a world class athlete. You won't find anyone who's mastered their sport without first learning the correct techniques and then practicing them regularly.

The good news is that you don't need a natural ability to master media interviews. There's also no need to practice every day like an athlete does but you do need to learn the techniques and put them into practice regularly to maintain the skills.

This book gives you those techniques but it'll be up to you to put them into practice. I can't emphasise enough how important this is. By reading this book you'll gain an intellectual understanding of how to face media interviews with confidence. You'll know the theory. The next step is putting it into practice.

You'll also know your role when it comes to crisis communication. Whether you have public relations staff or not, you need to play a major part in this. Your attitude towards preparation and decision making on crisis day will largely determine how your organisation fares if the unthinkable happens.

At the end of each chapter you'll find a specific section. This is purely focused on what's changed in the digital age that affects your dealings with the media. This is important because a failure to recognise these changes can damage your reputation.

How to read the book

The best way to read this book initially is from cover to cover. That's because your ability to face the media with confidence is dependent on understanding and mastering every part of the process. For this reason, missing out a chapter won't help you to complete the puzzle.

Once completed, you can then go back to specific chapters. For example, if you have a media interview approaching, you may wish to refresh your memory about how to create effective sound bites or you may organise a meeting with your public relations staff to discuss crisis communication and you could then read that specific chapter to prepare yourself for the meeting.

In a nutshell, once read, the book can become your media relations reference manual.

CHAPTER ONE

My perspective
from both sides of
the interview

CHAPTER ONE

My perspective from both sides of the interview

From my background on both sides of the media fence, I believe the best way to impress media audiences is to help those who are writing or producing the stories. This won't always be possible but as a rule, it's a good strategy.

> ## "Never pick a fight with people who buy ink by the barrel."
>
> 💬 **Mark Twain**

Helping journalists do their job well means that they are more likely to give you favourable coverage. If you refuse to talk or fail to give them good information, they'll be forced to look elsewhere for sources. They'll also be more likely to take a negative angle towards your organisation.

Most forms of media publicity are good for business. It's just a matter of knowing how to get your message across in a way that satisfies both you and your interviewer. Media interviews should be opportunities, not threats. Even if your organisation is in the midst of some emergency, expressing messages of empathy for victims and explaining what you are doing for them can have a positive impact on your reputation.

You may be highly sceptical about this and have a fear of facing the media. I don't blame you. I did too. When I moved from journalist to media advisor, I soon realised how difficult it was to be on the other side of the interview.

While I was comfortable with my media advisory role, my back-up spokesperson duties were entirely different. The first time I was on the record with a reporter, I was tongue-tied. I was concerned about the angle the reporter would take. It wasn't even a long interview because as back-up, I would never get into any major detail. I felt totally unprepared and at the mercy of the reporter. I was in a panic. I gave boring answers that did little to help the reporter.

Until that moment, I had no appreciation of how stressful this could be. It soon became very clear that just because I knew how to ask tough questions didn't mean I had any idea how to answer them. I learnt the ropes very quickly.

The sleepless nights wondering what that headline will read the next day is real to those dealing with the media when the stakes are high. The threat of being taken out of context is the most common concern I hear among my media training clients. There are ways to minimise the likelihood of this and these will be covered later in the book.

On the other side of the camera is the journalist whose job is dependent on filing good stories. That was my only consideration and that's understandable. That's the role of a journalist. But what I never thought about were the consequences for those I was interviewing if they said the wrong thing, I took an unfair angle or I misquoted them.

However, the best way to avoid these outcomes is to cooperate as much as possible. Despite views to the contrary, most journalists are not out to get you. They need good information from you that's packaged in the right way. That should be your aim. Obviously you won't always be able to tell them everything but if you can understand what they want and how to package it a way that helps them create an interesting story, everyone wins.

This book is focused on creating that win-win situation. You get your message out and both you and your interviewer get to impress readers, viewers or listeners.

How to handle approaches from the media

CHAPTER TWO

How to handle approaches from the media

When someone from a media outlet wants to talk to you about a story idea, this will usually begin with a telephone call. This could be from a journalist, producer or researcher from the outlet concerned.

Most of the time this call will be requesting an interview with you as a source for a story but sometimes the person will only want advice on where to find specific information. It may also be a call to assess your suitability as a source for the story.

If an interview request is made, there are some important steps to follow. Firstly, you need to find out as much as you can about the likely make-up of the story.

Your first question should be, "What is your intended focus?" This may mildly irritate the caller because they may not know what focus to take until all sources have been interviewed but it's an important question to ask otherwise you may go into an interview having little knowledge of what to expect.

Sometimes the focus of the story will be obvious. For example, you are a property investor and a reporter wants to know your views on a new government tax imposed on landlords. But what if you were asked to comment on a story a reporter was writing about workplace bullying? If you don't ask for more information, you won't know whether it's a general story looking at the views of multiple business owners or a specific story looking at a complaint one of your workers has made against you.

It's true, the caller may not tell you everything but most are happy to share this information. They won't give you the questions but they will give you a general idea.

You also need to know who else is being interviewed. If it's for print, you need to know if it's a long feature or a short news story. This will influence how you prepare.

The last thing you must always do is buy yourself some time. Never, ever do an interview on the spot. Use some excuse like, "I'm in a meeting at the moment, can I call you back in 15 minutes?" Make sure you do call back if you agree to do so.

Should you do the interview?

I'm a big believer that you should accept the request in most situations. The third party endorsement that a story in traditional media gives you is priceless. In these days of social media, many people and businesses use their own networks to get news out rather than look to official media outlets to share their messages.

While this is good to do, it doesn't offer the same credibility that a story in the local newspaper or nightly television news does. This point is often overlooked.

However, obviously not all stories are positive. There will be times when the news media can damage your reputation just as much as it can enhance it. This means that you must evaluate every media interview opportunity with caution before you accept. I think there must be a very good reason not to agree to an interview. Even if it is a negative issue, you may need to take the opportunity to state your case. Otherwise the story may be angled strongly against you. Before you decide, there are some important questions to ask.

Are you qualified?

While most media outlets will do their homework to decide whether you are suitable, they can get this wrong. For example, if you're a well-known lawyer, you could be asked to comment on a civil case that has just been through the courts but you may be a specialist in criminal law, not civil law. When this happens, you are best not to comment but make sure you tell the reporter why. The last thing you want in the story is a sentence saying that you refused to comment. It's also good practice to suggest a better person who does have that specialty.

Is it a negative issue you would rather not be associated with?

Reporters often search for comments from relevant sources on a topical issue. This can be positive. For example, your local sports team may have just won a major tournament and the local reporter wants to know how local businesses plan to celebrate. That would be fantastic free publicity for your business.

But what if that local reporter was canvassing regional schools after a spate of bullying episodes at one particular college? As a school principal, would you want to be involved in a story like that? This is something to think about. I wouldn't rule out the possibility of being involved. It could give you an opportunity to share your commitment to the problem with the local community but there is obviously a risk that the reporter will focus on any problems your school has faced. Your decision on this may depend on what sort of relationship you have with the reporter writing the story.

Will you be seen as the villain regardless?

Sometimes it's clear that you will be seen as a villain, despite what you may say. For example, after failing to pay an electricity account for three months and after four warnings, an elderly war veteran has had his power turned off. As the CEO of the electricity company, you are asked to appear on a television show with the man. The audience will side with the war veteran's plight and you will be seen as responsible.

In these situations, you may feel that little will be gained from appearing. This will need careful consideration. If you don't front up, you lose the opportunity to defend your position and it could also appear as if you are guilty.

Decisions about whether to appear in such circumstances must be made on a case-by-case basis.

What if your lawyer advises against it?

Obviously, you need to listen to your lawyer. There will be times when you can't comment. For example, something may be before the courts and you would be breaking sub judice. There will also be times when your lawyer advises you not to talk, even if it's legal to do so. When this happens, think very carefully and seek advice from a public relations practitioner to balance up that advice. The reason for this is the distinct difference between the court of law and the court of public opinion. Lawyers are concerned with the court of law and keeping you out of jail but you must also consider the court of public opinion. If your failure to comment damages your reputation, you may no longer have a viable business. The court of public opinion is quite different from a court of law.

Basically, you are guilty until proven innocent, while the court of law works in reverse. If a news story says that you refused to comment, research shows that most people think you have something to hide. You need to give this strong consideration if ever placed in this situation.

Could you send a statement only?

Leaders often like to send the media a statement rather than taking part in a media interview. Sometimes this can work but broadcasting media won't like this idea for obvious reasons. Television is a visual medium so television reporters will want you on camera. While sending a statement is an option, it can also work against you. If you go on camera, you get a far better opportunity to put your case. There's also no guarantee your statement will get used.

But if you feel you'd be on a hiding to nothing, you can consider a statement. Your decision can also depend on whether it's for a two minute news story or a detailed feature piece. If it's the latter, a three sentence statement will pale into insignificance, as the rest of the piece is likely to be filled by your detractors.

Radio will also want to talk to you because they rely on audio. The same principles that apply to television apply to radio.

Print media are sometimes more open to a statement but before considering it, you need to understand the negatives involved. Firstly, it's not great for developing a relationship with the reporter. The better your relationship with the reporter, the better the coverage you will get. This doesn't mean you'll always get great publicity but the reporter will always give you a fair hearing. That's all you can ever ask for.

The other negative is that your point of view may only be represented by a few sentences while those who participate in an interview are likely to dominate the column centimetres. However, if it's for a 300 word news story, your view would probably only receive a brief quote or two anyway. In this case, the statement approach could work to your advantage. I always encourage those who send in statements to make them short. That way, you can almost guarantee that everything you write will get used. It's important that your statement includes key points and a few sound bites. Remember, you still need to give the reporter good material that can help her write an interesting story.

In a nutshell, if it's a negative news story for a print publication and the reporter is happy, a statement is fine. For broadcasting, only ever consider a statement if you feel you're on a hiding to nothing by agreeing to an interview.

Could you agree to live interviews only?

Later in the book I'll explain how to avoid having your words taken out of context. This is a fear many people have with media interviews, particularly when the stakes are high. For example, let's say you are the CEO of a large building company that's been in existence for 50 years and a reporter asks you, "How many accidents has your company had on building sites?" That sounds like a reasonable question. You may answer, "We've had 25 accidents, they have all been minor and we haven't had one for the last 20 years."

The problem here is that the reporter may only take the first part of that answer which would make your business look accident prone. It could then be compared with other companies that have only been in existence for a few years.

If the stakes are high and you've seen the reporter do this sort of thing before, you would understandably be nervous. Rather than declining the interview, you could agree to do it live only. That's assuming the request has come from a broadcasting outlet and they do present live interviews. That way, there's little chance for the footage of you to be sliced and diced to make you look incompetent.

One thing you need to bear in mind with this is that parts of your live interview can be cut up for later news bulletins. However, at least this way people who see the live interview will understand. You are also less likely to be taken out of context in this way because people who see both the interview and future bulletins will see the disparity.

What if it is a major crisis causing death or serious injury?

In these situations, it's important that you do comment and you do it quickly. In the above example about the war veteran, it was clear that you would be seen as the villain. When a crisis erupts, the media and public decide early on whether you are the villain or another victim. If you fail to front up, your chances of being portrayed as the villain rise sharply.

> # "Four hostile newspapers are more to be feared than a thousand bayonets."
>
> ### 💬 **Napoléon Bonaparte**

In the early stages of a crisis causing death or serious injury, you don't need all the answers but you do need to show empathy and communicate what you are doing to help the situation. This is such a crucial part of media relations that I have a chapter dedicated to it later in the book.

How to turn down the request

If you do turn down the interview request, your approach will depend on the credibility of your reason. If you have a good reason that would be understood by the audience of the media outlet concerned, use it. For example, if it was before the courts, you could say, "I'd like to help but the case is before the courts and I am unable to talk about it publicly."

You may also decide to decline for moral reasons. A reporter may want to talk to you about staff morale a few weeks after you have to lay off 10 workers. You could say something like, "Out of respect for those we had to let go and the hurt it caused other workers, I'd rather keep our feelings out of the public spotlight."

However, if the reason for failing to front wouldn't be accepted as credible, don't give a reason. Let's say a staff member of yours was killed in a workplace accident and you decide you can't face the media because you've been up for 30 hours straight. If you said you couldn't talk because you're too tired, the story could read something like, "Boss too tired to talk about worker's death."

In a serious situation like this, you should be fronting media to show empathy for the victim's family and friends but if you did decide to turn it down, just say you are unavailable. Don't give any more information and never lie.

No comment

You may have noticed here that I've never used the words, 'no comment.' When you don't want to answer a journalist's questions, these are usually the first two words that come to mind for most of us but they are the last two words you should ever use when talking to the media. That's because they automatically ring alarm bells in the reporter's head. Whenever they're used, the reporter and anyone else hearing or seeing them thinks the user has something to hide. You never want to give that impression.

There are better ways. Take the workplace accident example above. Clearly the boss couldn't say he was too tired or 'no comment' but what he could have said, either personally, through email or through someone else was, "I'm unable to talk to you now but what I can say is that my heart goes out to the family of the victim."

This way he has avoided using the words, 'no comment.' He also comes across as caring and gives the reporter at least something to use in the story. In a situation like this, it would be advisable to tell the reporter when you will be able to talk.

Agreeing to talk "off the record"

The expression "off the record" has different meanings to different people. One of these is a willingness for someone to give a reporter information but on the proviso that the source is not named in the story. There are many reasons people do this. It could be a whistle-blower in an organisation who wants to get something into the public arena but it would be detrimental to her career if she was named. Politicians sometimes give reporters information that can embarrass their opponents but it would look bad if people knew where it had come from. The same applies to business executives who want information revealed about competitors.

The reporter would be expected to quote the source but in a way that couldn't identify her. For example, "A source close to the President" or "A senior insider." There are many options, depending on the situation. If you do agree to this, you need to make sure you can't be identified. It's important that you're one of many possible sources. For example, if you were a member of parliament for a small party where there were only two males, you wouldn't want to be named as a male from that party.

If the pool of possible sources is too small, others in the pool may be uncomfortable and even come out publicly to say it wasn't them.

The other meaning of "off the record" is when you don't give permission for the reporter to use your name or the information you are giving. This is often used to provide a context for the reporter to understand the issue at hand. If the reporter then wants to use that information, she'll have to find someone else prepared to be named as the source of that information.

When it comes to giving information "off the record," only ever contemplate it if you have total trust in the reporter. I've given material to a reporter but it was someone I knew extremely well and I had no doubt whatsoever that he would keep his word.

Before doing so, there are a few things you need to understand. Firstly, make it abundantly clear what type of "off the record" definition you are agreeing to. Secondly, remember that the person you are talking to is probably a reporter who has an editor or producer to answer to. While unlikely, that person may demand that the source is revealed. This becomes more important when the information is of a highly sensitive nature.

If you have any doubt whatsoever, don't go "off the record." If you don't trust the reporter with your life, if you believe the pool of possible sources is too small or the information is highly sensitive and could put pressure on the reporter to reveal your name, don't do it. Lots of media advisors will tell you never to contemplate doing this. I think there is a place for it but be careful. I can also tell you from experience that it can be extremely nerve-wracking when the information you gave is published or broadcast. This is particularly so if you are an obvious suspect.

What about an ambush interview?

One risk you take when turning down an interview request is the potential for an ambush interview. This is where a reporter approaches you unannounced and barrages you with questions. These are more common for television reporters accompanied by a cameraman because they make great pictures.

You'll have seen them. It could be a businessman being chased by a reporter or aggressively placing a hand over the camera lens while telling the cameraman to stop filming.

This usually happens because a reporter can't get hold of you any other way but there are also other reasons. A deadline may be fast approaching and a television reporter desperately wants a comment from you before her deadline.

The other most likely possibility is a reporter walking down the street or into local businesses taking a snap poll or asking for comment on a specific issue. This could be positive or negative.

If the ambush is because you've proved elusive, you can expect it to be more aggressive. Also, be aware that your reaction to the ambush will determine the angle of the subsequent story. If you get aggressive or emotional, your behaviour will become the story. The same will happen if you try to run away or place your hand over the camera.

The first thing to do in this situation is remain calm. You should politely tell the reporter you are happy to talk but now is not a good time. Organise a convenient time but remain calm throughout. If you take that approach, there's no interesting footage to use for the television news but it's important that you stick to your word and meet at the agreed time and location.

If the approach is less aggressive and the reporter does want a quick quote on an important issue before a fast approaching deadline, you should still buy some time. This could be as little as five minutes. You need to give it some thought and get your head in the right space. If you don't feel you can do justice to your comment in that time, politely tell the reporter you'd be happy to talk another time but you don't feel comfortable under the current circumstances.

The same goes for the snap poll or comment on a specific issue but these issues are likely to be far less controversial than the one involving the source who has been ambushed as a last resort.

What's changed in the digital age?

One job you must do now is a quick google search of the reporter who will be interviewing you. This was difficult before the digital age. Merely plug the name into google and have a look at the reporter's earlier stories. This will help you to understand the approach she usually takes. For example, is she aggressive? Is she a specialist on the topic? This only needs to take a minute.

The amount of time you can buy before your interview has dropped dramatically. The reporter may place a version of the story on the media outlet website before you have even been interviewed. If you take too long to get back to her, the story will be on the site and out through social media channels without your comments. Although you will be represented in an updated version of the story, you will have lost the opportunity to influence the angle. Chances are that your comments will consist of a sentence or two at the very end of the story.

If you decide to turn down an interview request, be aware that the issue is probably being discussed at length on social media. If it's something you're at the centre of, you may need to reconsider if you turned down the request. Stories or issues can be totally one-sided. Sometimes it's because the reporter or producer decided to take that focus but it's usually because the spokesperson refused to front. If this is the case, you can't complaint about the story being slanted in a particular direction. If you are not available to put your side of the argument, how can you blame the reporter for producing a one-sided story?

This becomes even more crucial when it gets into social media because the media not only sends out stories through social media, they also use it as a major source of information and sound bites. There will be plenty of negative posts on Twitter and other networks that will make fantastic quotes for reporters.

Dealing with bloggers

The explosion of blogs throughout the world is another phenomenon in the digital age. This means that the chances are high that you'll be approached for comment by bloggers, just as you will from journalists.

Most of the principles to follow here are the same but there are a few extra precautions you must take when you receive such requests. Find out if the blog has a specific focus. For example, many have a political leaning so if you are a known Liberal Party supporter and the blog is known for its aggressive anti-liberal stance, you may choose to stay away.

While some media outlets also have political slants, remember that bloggers are not subject to as much ethical control as journalists so it's important to do your research.

Some leaders tend to ignore blogs that have a small readership. This can also be the case with small media outlets but remember that getting your points across to any audience can be an opportunity rather than a threat. Most blogs are niche so won't always have a huge circulation but if that niche is your market, the publicity can be good for business.

Preparing your media message

CHAPTER THREE

Preparing your media message

Most people who come to my media training sessions are more concerned about how to answer difficult questions than what they want to say. What they don't understand is that a media interview is between two people. The reporter asks the questions but what they forget is that you have total control of how you answer them. As I mentioned earlier, it's best to help the reporter as much as possible. However, it is also important that you have points that you want to get across to the audience.

You have just as much right to contribute to what is discussed during the interview. Obviously, the reporter comes up with the topic but you can then come up with points you want to focus on that are relevant to the topic.

If you don't do this, what's your aim for the interview? Clearly you wouldn't have one. So, preparing these points is vital if you're to create an opportunity from the interview. Otherwise your plan can only be one of survival and placing yourself at the mercy of the reporter.

Once you have bought some time and know what topic your interviewer wants to focus on, it's time to prepare. If you're new to the process of media interviews, this section may seem surprising because a media interview is unlike any other conversation you will ever have. That means the preparation must be different.

Media messages

Your first task should always be to create a media message. That consists of the three most important points you want to get across in your interview. All three points should be as brief as possible, lasting no more than 25 seconds combined. That's just over 8 seconds for each point or one sentence. The best way to understand the elements of a media message are through my CIB Formula. This acronym stands for Clarity, Interest and Brevity.

Clarity

The first element of your media message is clarity. The points must be as clear as possible. Remember that people get thousands of messages every day which means that most of those will be forgotten. Only the ones that are clear and easily understood will be remembered. This means that the simplest words should be used. For example, instead of 'endeavour' use 'try' and instead of saying 'at this present point in time' use 'now.'

Some people think that by using big words, others will think of them as more credible experts but the opposite is true. Just think of the great communicators of the past. Winston Churchill and John F Kennedy were great orators but always used the simplest of language.

> ## "Short words are the best and old words, when short, are the best of all."
>
> 💬 **Winston Churchill**

Even if people do understand the bigger word, it still takes their brain longer to process it. If you want them to understand your message as quickly as possible, use the most basic words you can think of.

Also think about the audience of the media outlet that the story will be appearing in. Is it a general audience? We occasionally all fall into the trap of assuming that others understand everything we take for granted. Industry jargon is a classic example. Never use acronyms unless you know they're widely known. I train many leaders in the education industry and they use industry jargon all the time. It's easy to assume everyone understands their jargon because that's the world they live in. What about you?

You can relax a bit more if the media outlet is focused on a specific industry or group of people but even then, don't take this for granted. There will still be people reading that publication or following that broadcast who don't have the level of knowledge that you possess. The best way to play it safe is to look at back issues of the publication or archives of the broadcast programme where the story will appear. This will show you how sophisticated your message should be. If you don't have time for this, remember that newspapers are written in a language that an 11-year-old can understand. Most business publications are also written for the layman rather than the expert.

Interest

The second vital element in your media message must be interest. It must be appealing to the audience of the media outlet that your interviewer is representing. Failure to recognise this is a common mistake. The journalist won't be impressed if your points are all self-centred and you fail to take the audience into account. It'll put major pressure on her. Remember that she's employed to produce interesting stories, not act as your free public relations officer.

Once you've constructed your media message, it's a good idea to show it to someone outside your area of expertise. Make sure that the person is within the target market of the media outlet that will publish or broadcast the story.

It's a common mistake to think that something of interest to us will automatically be of interest to everyone else. Think of some of your friends who talk about things that they're passionate about but you have no interest in. We accept that from friends but not from media outlets. If we start reading a story and quickly lose interest in it, we move on. The reporter's job is to keep us reading. That's also your job.

Brevity

I've already covered how brief your message must be. This is because media formats are all brief. If your points are much longer, they'll either be ignored or cut into smaller chunks that may not be understandable. Remember that the average time for a sound bite on television or radio news is about seven seconds. That's why we need to keep our points brief, even if it takes time to prepare.

> ## "I'm sorry I wrote you such a long letter. I didn't have time to write you a short one."
>
> 💬 **Attributed to both Mark Twain and Blaise Pascal**

Your interview plan

Your plan for the interview is to make these points the focus of the story, whether for print, radio, television or the internet.

This is achieved by coming back to them throughout your interview but this doesn't mean you need to repeat them word for word. As long as they've got the same meaning, you can say them in a number of ways. We'll look at this in the next chapter when we focus on sound bites.

By adopting this approach, the journalist is far more likely to use your points. Remember that most news stories only cover a few points, so by coming back to yours in different ways, you dramatically increase the chances of them making it into the final story. If you give the reporter

50 points, she'll whittle them down to two or three because that's all she has the time or space for. You may talk to the reporter for 30 minutes but unless the interview is live, you are likely to see one or possibly two sentences of what you said survive into the subsequent story. So if you give the reporter 50 different points to choose from, you lose any control over what ends up in the story but if you focus on just three, your chances are pretty good that your points will make the cut. Of course, this doesn't mean you don't answer the questions asked of you but we'll focus on that in a later chapter.

What types of message points are there?

Once you understand the CIB of media messages, they can still be difficult to build. Here are some examples of the types of message points that are often used. This isn't a complete set but they'll be helpful if you find it difficult to build your message. Remember that these examples are all individual points. Your three point media message can contain a variety of these, or others that you come up with yourself.

Stating a problem and its cause

This message point defines a problem and suggests what the cause may be. Here are two examples.

- Developing nations are emitting more CO^2 than ever before because there is no incentive to reduce them.

- Poverty levels throughout the OECD are rising because governments aren't doing enough to help people at the bottom of the income ladder.

Providing a solution to a problem

This is similar to the last message point type. They both highlight a problem but this one offers a solution rather than suggest a cause.

- The government could solve the chronic shortage of health service funding by increasing the taxes on cigarettes and alcohol.
- People with no qualifications would find it easier to get a job if they enrolled in a training course.

Call to action

These messages tell your audience to do something.

- If you really want the government to increase the unemployment benefit, call your local MP and demand action.
- Anyone serious about quitting smoking should contact their GP immediately to find out about all the options they've got to help kick the habit.

How you can help

By all means tell the audience how you can help but make sure it's relevant to the topic at hand. It'd also be advisable to limit this to one message point per interview unless the topic is specifically about how you can help.

- Anyone who suffers from this chronic illness could sign up for our free two month trial.

- Anyone who wants cheap flights this Christmas should book these through our website as early as possible.

Results or achievements

Don't be too modest when it comes to media interviews. If your results or achievements would be of interest to the audience, go ahead and mention them. As above, it wouldn't be advisable to have this focus with all three points.

- Since our restaurant opened last year, we've given all our leftover food to homeless people.
- By using our online booking service, business owners save time and get the most competitive prices

Messages when crisis strikes

The message points above are generally used for any media issue that's not a crisis and there are no victims. When there are victims, I always recommend that my media training clients use the three points below as a starting point. This is particularly important at the outset of a crisis or emergency.

Often, little information is available at this point but it's important to communicate what you can without getting into trouble by speculating. In a nutshell, these points allow you to do three things. Firstly, show empathy, secondly, explain what you are doing to help and thirdly, if possible, offer some reassurance.

Realistically, there'll be little more you can say at this point but it's important that you do front. The best approach is to look at it from the point of view of those affected. What would they want to know? Obviously, you will communicate whatever facts you can but otherwise, these three points will show that you care and you're doing all you can for the victims. These are the attributes people look for during times of crisis.

Regret or Empathy

This is the most important point to include in your message if you are dealing with an issue where there are victims. This could be anything from the death of a staff member to laying off workers. Empathy is often overlooked as a message point and can make spokespeople look insensitive if they ignore it. It's important to remember that a statement of empathy doesn't have to be an apology. All it does is show some warmth to those affected. Lawyers can be nervous about expressing empathy in some situations but it can be simply done without admitting fault. For example:

- Our hearts go out to the victim's family after this tragic accident
- I offer my sincere condolences to everyone we've had to lay off today and their families

Response

Where a negative event like those mentioned above occurs, the second point in your message should be what you're doing to help. People expect you to be doing everything you can, so you need to show them that you're doing exactly that. The response point can be more abstract than others, as long as examples of what you're doing is also mentioned. We'll come to this later when we look at sound bites and different ways of expressing your points.

- We're doing everything we can to support the family and friends of the victim
- We'll help the workers deal with the shock of this news and do all we can to find them new jobs

Reassurance

This is what I call the third R in my recommended crisis media message. People want reassurance that everything will work out well. Obviously, this'll never be the case for a family if a loved one has been killed but for everyone else, they'll be concerned about their own safety or the safety of loved ones.

Reassurance is also important for other serious issues like layoffs. The decision whether to use it or not will depend on whether it can be given.

- We'll launch a full scale review of our safety procedures
- The safety of our staff has always been our number one priority. (This may not be the most attractive point for media to use but there'll be better ways of expressing it in the form of sound bites. These will be covered in the next chapter.)

Brainstorming session

Sometimes media messages are simple to come up with. There are three clear things you want to say and they fit nicely into your message but sometimes it's difficult. It could be complex issues you're dealing with or you may have so much to say that you find it impossible to break it down into three points.

The answer is a brainstorming session with a colleague. Write down all the possible points you could make and start analysing. You'll probably find that some of the points are quite similar, while others will get struck out early in the process.

Developing your message becomes simpler the more you do it. You may also find that your media interviews are usually on similar topics. This means you may only need to tweak existing messages for a new interview but it's vital that you spend time getting your message right. It doesn't have to take more than 10 minutes to complete. When you've done it once, you'll realise how important it is because there's no other way of knowing what you want to get across in the interview. By having your media message prepared, you have a plan and a goal for the interview.

In most cases, a media interview is an opportunity to grow your reputation, your media profile and often your business bottom line so you need to take time to prepare.

Let me put this another way. If you had a big presentation to deliver to hundreds of people, would you prepare? The only difference here is that the media interview is likely to reach many thousands of people, not just a few hundred.

Most people don't prepare because they think it takes too much time. This is no excuse. Unless live, a media interview will last as long as it takes for the reporter to get what she wants. By preparing points that'll benefit you and give her a good story, you may only need to speak to her for a few minutes. In contrast, I once had an untrained person telephone me, excited that a television crew had been with him for three hours. He thought this was a good thing but it took them that long to get what they needed. When the story aired, his input was a single sound bite. So, preparing won't only help you get a better outcome, it'll save you time.

What's changed in the digital age?

The big change in the digital age is the reduction in the time you have to make your point. It wasn't long ago that some media trainers told their clients to keep their media messages to no more than 60 seconds but in the digital age, the length of news stories has reduced significantly.

People don't want to read or watch detailed news stories. They have so many choices for news these days that they're very selective. They also have far more information directed at them on a daily basis and that's why they want stories to be short and sharp. As a result, news outlets have reduced the length of their stories.

This is why your media messages should be no longer than 25 seconds. If they're longer, they'll be less attractive to the media and it also increases the chance of journalists paraphrasing them. This can lead to mistakes and the risk that they'll change the context of your message without knowing it.

Make your message more media friendly

CHAPTER FOUR

Make your message more media friendly

The best media communicators know exactly what journalists want and how to give it to them. They don't just relay their message points, they take it a step further. They dress them up in ways that make them more memorable, more interesting and more attractive to journalists. That heavily raises the odds of them making it into the story. Let's look at a few well known examples.

"Mr Gorbechev, tear down that wall." Ronald Reagan.

"We will fight them on the beaches." Winston Churchill.

"If the glove doesn't fit, you must acquit." OJ Simpson's Defence Lawyer.

As you'll be aware, these weren't all made in media interviews but they all made it past media gatekeepers and into the news because they were all such unique ways of making a point. We all know that the news media staff have the final say in what material makes it into edited news stories but if you dress your points up like this, you have a major influence over what they decide to use. This is another good example of why helping the journalist is usually the best way of helping yourself.

Sound bites

You've seen or heard sound bites in broadcast news bulletins and direct quotes in written media stories. These are the short clips from spokespeople that are used verbatim and they usually last anywhere from 5 to 15 seconds. On television news programmes, you see and hear them, on radio you hear them, while in print media you read them between the speech marks. The average length continues to drop as media stories keep getting shorter in detail. My last estimation was an average time of about seven seconds.

Journalists need good sound bites and quotes for their stories. It helps bring them to life and makes them more real to audiences. This gives you a great opportunity as a spokesperson. It means if you package the points from your media messages in unique and interesting ways, they are bound to survive the editing process and appear in the story as sound bites or quotes.

Take the Winston Churchill sound bite above as an example. That was taken out of an emotional speech he was giving. The point he wanted to make was that Britain wouldn't accept defeat in World War Two but by making the point in a far more interesting way, "We will fight them on the beaches," his emotive language not only gave reporters a fantastic sound bite to bring their stories to life but it got his point across to his audience in a memorable way that they wouldn't forget.

You can do the same. It's just a matter of understanding exactly what elements journalists look for in their sound bites, then you can come up with your own ones that make your key points in unique and interesting ways. By mastering this and knowing how to get them across, you'll come as close as you can possibly get to writing or producing the story yourself.

Time to prepare

Creating ear catching sound bites is an extra layer in the preparation process for media interviews. It's easy to ignore and just focus on your three key points. This is entirely up to you but there are a few things you must bear in mind first. If you create them properly, you won't be disappointed. The journalist will thank you and you can sleep easy knowing they'll probably be used in the following morning's newspaper.

They also help you avoid sounding like a broken record. This is always a concern of my media training clients. Creating great sound bites is the best way to avoid this and keep focused on your message.

We've all seen media interviews where the spokesperson rattles off exactly the same line after every question. This damages credibility but if you have different and interesting ways of repeating the same points, (after answering the question briefly), your credibility will grow.

They'll be remembered

Another important benefit of crafting your own sound bites is that they'll be remembered. We're all bombarded with thousands of messages every day. Think how many come through your email, work conversations, advertisements and social and traditional media. How many of those messages do you remember? Not many. Our brains can't cope with many and it selects the most interesting ones. You need your points to make this cut. Crafting interesting sound bites for your interviews is the way to do that. If you don't, your points may go in one ear and straight out the other.

George Bernard Shaw knew how difficult it was to get messages across when he made the following profound statement.

> # "The single biggest problem with communication is the illusion that it has taken place."

Shaw's quote recognises that communication isn't just sending a message to someone. To count as communication, it must also register with the intended target. Turning points into interesting sound bites is a great way to make that happen.

This need for interesting sound bites becomes even more necessary if your message points are important but the topic is quite mundane. You need to bring your points to life. If you don't, the reporter may not continue with the story and if he does, it may well get little attention from readers, viewers or listeners and you will have lost an opportunity.

A warning about sound bites

Crafting and communicating good sound bites can not only help you get your message across but they can also work against you. Reporters always look for great sound bites or quotes but this doesn't mean they'll always portray you in a favourable light. If you say something that could be used against you in an interesting way, that's just as likely to be used as a sound bite.

You may remember the Gulf of Mexico oil spill of 2010. BP CEO Tony Hayward made some interesting remarks that were taken out of context to make him look out of touch and selfish. At one point he was asked how the whole ordeal was affecting him. Amongst a detailed answer, he used the words, "I want my life back." That was used as a sound bite by media across the world. It was taken out of context and didn't portray what he meant but he said it so it was fair game.

Later in the book I'll discuss the importance of avoiding negative language. However, while we are discussing sound bites, it's important to understand that statements of denial make popular sound bites although they rarely work for the person using them. Just ask former American President Bill Clinton when he said, "I did not have sexual relations with that woman."

Another former US President will also wish he never used a denial statement. During a speech after the Watergate scandal, Richard Nixon told the audience that he had worked for every cent he owned and he was proud of what he'd done as president. The words following that would become one of the most famous sound bites ever used. It's still used today. The four famous words were "I'm not a crook."

That trumped everything else in his speech and was the focus of media attention for years to come. It's also the lasting memory many people have of him.

So while sound bites can be your greatest ally, they can also be your worst enemy. We want to help reporters as much as possible but not at our own expense.

The RACES sound bite formula

So how do you craft your own sound bites? Below is a list of 11 elements that are often found in the sound bites and quotes chosen by reporters. Sometimes more than one of these appear in a single sound bite. My RACES formula by no means covers every sound bite ever used but it's a fairly comprehensive list you can use as a guide to crafting your own. You can even take some of the actual examples and tailor them to your specific interview topics.

Rhymes

This isn't one of the most common elements used in sound bites but when it's used, it can be powerful. I've already mentioned the words used by OJ Simpson's lawyer. He said, "If the glove doesn't fit, you must acquit." That uses a rhyme in the best possible way. It's a far more attractive way of communicating the point that if the glove wasn't the size worn by OJ Simpson, he couldn't be found guilty. There are easier elements to use in forming sound bites but if any interesting rhymes come to mind, they're well worth considering.

Rhetorical questions

These are often simple to come up with. Sometimes it's just a matter of slightly rewording a message point. For example, in the last chapter when we discussed media messages, I emphasised the need to show empathy in a crisis where there's a victim. The example point I used was, "Our hearts go out to the family of the victim." A rhetorical question sound bite could easily be created from that. This could read, "Wouldn't anyone sympathise with a family who had received such devastating news?"

That makes the same point but in a more interesting way. This would allow the journalist to add some variety to the structure of the story.

Analogies

Journalists like using analogies because they also add variety to a story. Analogies are always interesting because they explain something by relating it to something else everyone understands. For example, a businesswoman might be interviewed about why her business has performed better than her competition in a difficult economic climate.

One of her points might be that she doesn't want to give away too much financial information because that could help her competitors learn valuable lessons about her secrets. She could make that point in a more interesting way by using an analogy.

For example, she could say, "Giving you that information for my competitors to see would be like the Brazilian football team giving Germany their game plan before next week's World Cup Final." Which one do you think the reporter would use and which one would people remember?

Absolutes

These are simple to craft. They just involve making points that are unqualified. They could be a guarantee of something, a 100 percent commitment or even a point that merely includes the word 'absolute' in it. George H Bush used one of these when making the point that he would not raise taxes. Instead of using the point, "There will be no new taxes," the sound bite that got used was, "Read my lips. No new taxes." That was simple, clear and unqualified.

Conflict

The use of conflict is popular with reporters and media audiences. It brings a story to life. Clearly there's a time and a place for it but if your interview involves an issue you're angry or unhappy about, conflict is a worthy consideration. Just make sure it won't backfire on you. The Winston Churchill sound bite mentioned earlier is a perfect example of the use of conflict. His point was that Britain would never be defeated by Nazi Germany. He said, "We will fight them on the beaches."

Clichés

Clichés are a great way to make a point. Some people say they should be avoided but the reason they became clichés in the first place was because they were a great way to make a particular point. However, there are a few things to bear in mind before using them. Firstly, they must be clichés that are widely known. Just because you're aware of one doesn't mean everyone is but if it passes that test, it can form a great sound bite. The second consideration is that it must be adapted to your scenario. For example, you may want to make the point that a building you have under construction will take some time to complete but when the final brick is laid, it will be stunning. You could use the cliché, "Rome wasn't built in a day" but you don't want to leave it there. You need to add your context to it. For example, "Rome wasn't built in a day but once this building is completed, everyone will see that it was well worth the wait."

Comedy

Comedy will get used almost every time by a journalist and there are many ways it can be used in sound bites. Often it's linked with an analogy or a simile. You need to be extra careful with comedy because what may be hilarious to one person could be highly offensive to another. The best practice is to err on the side of caution. Let's say a government has just decided against a tax cut it had planned because economic conditions changed.

A member of that government could have as a message point, "I've got mixed feelings about this because I believe in tax cuts but we're in difficult economic times." A sound bite focused on comedy to make this point could say, "This is a bit like my mother-in-law driving over a cliff in my brand new Porsche. I've got mixed feelings about it." I don't need to tell you which of those options is the most entertaining and has the ability to bring that story to life but did you think it was funny or highly offensive? Opinions are usually split.

Emotion

Reporters love using emotion in their stories but they can't use it in their own words. Humans love emotion and reporters know that, so how can you create sound bites that include an element of emotion? The key is to use emotive words like horrified, devastated, ecstatic or delighted. In the crisis message points discussed earlier, I mentioned that the first message point where there had been a victim should be one of regret or empathy. The example message point read, "Our hearts go out to the family of the victim." A sound bite using emotion in that scenario could simply be something like, "As a parent myself, I can understand that the victim's family must be devastated."

Examples

Examples are a great way to make a point because they often take an abstract point and turn it into something concrete. Remember that key points are the general themes we want to get across in our interviews. Sometimes these will be abstract in nature. For example, in the crisis media messages discussed in the last chapter, I suggested that the second key point could be your response. In other words, what you are doing to help. In that example, the point read, "We're doing everything we can to support the family and friends of the victim."

That's a fairly abstract point. It would certainly get your point across that you are responding as well as you can but examples will do the same job. Whether you use the abstract message point or actual examples of what you are doing, that same point is being made. An example of a sound bite in this scenario could simply be, "We have counsellors available around the clock for friends and family for as long as they're needed."

Statistics

Journalists like using statistics in their stories. They're similar to examples in the sense that they're concrete. There's nothing abstract about them. They make a point through hard data but you must be sure the statistics you use are credible. There's no point using them from an unscientific survey or one that only surveyed a few people as that would harm your credibility with the journalist.

Never overwhelm the reporter with statistics. You're best to use only one or perhaps two statistics as another way of making a point. For example, one of your message points could be that too many people are living below the poverty line.

If you had a relevant statistic to back up that point, it would make a valuable sound bite. For example (and I'm only using this fictional figure to make the point), you could say something like, "Over the last 12 months, the number of children living in poverty has doubled to reach 300,000."

Before you create sound bites with statistics, there's an important lesson to learn about them. Sometimes, and even in the example I've used above, a statistic may not mean much to people. The figure of 300,000 sounds big, but relative to what? In some situations, it'd be better to relate it to something people know about.

For example, the sound bite could be phrased this way, "The number of children living in poverty could fill Stadium Australia seven times over." That would have more impact because readers, viewers or listeners could then measure more clearly how many children you are talking about.

Similes

These are similar to analogies but there are differences. They are alike in the sense that they liken one thing to something else but analogies are logical arguments, where there is a real justification for the comparison. Similes relate things to make a point and are a figure of speech rather than an argument that the two things are realistically similar. They do this by using the words 'like' or 'as' to make their points. For example, a message point could be, "My staff put their own lives at risk to save those animals from certain death." A simile-focused sound bite could say, "It was only because my staff were as brave as lions that we got them all out alive."

Stories

When it comes to presentations, stories are without doubt the best way to get audiences to remember the points you're making. They're also effective in media interviews. The only difference is that those used in presentations can be far longer and more detailed. The best stories are based on personal experiences but they can also be things you've heard from others although you can also use hypothetical stories. If you do this, make sure it's clear to everyone that it's not true. The last thing people want is to hear an interesting story, only to be told at the end that it wasn't real. Let's look at how a personal story could be used as an effective sound bite. An opposition political party is against a government policy that's about to impose a new tax on small businesses. The message point could be, "This tax will cripple many small businesses because they're struggling to make ends meet already."

If the politician knew a business owner who said he'd close down if the new tax was introduced, that would make a great story. For example, "I met the owner of a small manufacturing company last week who said he'll lay off five workers as soon as this tax is introduced." That makes the same point and offers something concrete to the more abstract message point.

When you come up with your sound bites, place them on a sheet of paper below the message point they represent. This sheet will be your focus for the interview. If it's a telephone interview, have it in front of you. Just remember not to sound scripted. While you will return to your message points in different ways throughout your interview, only ever use a constructed sound bite once.

What's changed in the digital age?

Sound bites and quotes have got shorter. It doesn't seem that long since the average length of a sound bite was about 12 to 15 seconds. Now, it's seven seconds. This is because stories are shorter than they've ever been. People want their news to be as brief as possible. So, if your sound bites are too long, you'll struggle to get your points across in the time available.

This is important. If you take too long to make your points, journalists will have no choice but to cut your sound bites in half or paraphrase them. By cutting them in half, the context may change from what you intended and if they paraphrase, there's the risk that they'll get something wrong. If you make your sound bites clear, interesting and brief, everyone wins.

The need for brevity in the digital age isn't just a news media phenomenon. It's everywhere. Social media is a great example. Twitter posts can only be 140 characters.

In today's world there are so many messages competing for our attention which has made it a major challenge to get our points through to our intended targets and remembered. That's why you should use sound bite elements in other parts of your life. For example, if you want a Twitter post to be remembered, why not dress it up as a catchy sound bite? Why not make your big points in a board meeting using sound bite elements? You need to give people's brains a reason to hold onto that information. By using plain, mundane language, the chances are that your points will be forgotten almost immediately.

CHAPTER FIVE

Body Language speaks louder than words

CHAPTER FIVE

Body Language speaks louder than words

When you prepare for important conversations, whether they be meetings or television interviews, your focus is probably on what to say. However, what's just as important is your non-verbal communication. People will decide quickly whether they like you and trust you. They'll also decide how confident you are and whether you mean what you say. What's surprising is that their assessment has little to do with what you say but more about your body language.

I learnt this lesson the hard way. I was interviewed for a place on a highly sought after journalism course many years ago. I was well qualified for it. I had a good university degree and experience in a newsroom. I also had the support of a well-respected editor. Even though it was competitive, she thought I'd easily make the cut.

Then the interview began. I didn't think I mastered it but I thought it went well enough. I was wrong. When I received a letter in the mail saying I had missed out, I contacted the editor who had supported me. She was shocked and contacted the course director who told her that I'd come across as though I couldn't care less about whether I got into the course or not. In other words, what I said was fine but my body language gave the impression that I wasn't interested. Thankfully, my supporting editor managed to get me onto the shortlist for the course and I managed to get in after someone pulled out.

This wasn't a media interview but the same principles apply. How many times have you seen someone on television who you can't identify with? It's probably because what they're saying isn't matching their body language. A new politician may say she's delighted to have been elected but if she says it without smiling and in a monotone voice, people won't believe her. A business leader could be announcing that a worker's been killed in a freak accident but if he says his heart goes out to the family of the victim and there's no passion being shown by his facial expressions, people won't believe he's as sincere as his words suggest.

> ## "It's not what you say that matters. It's whether people believe you mean what you say."
>
> ### 🗩 Pete Burdon, 2015

Move those hands

If there's one thing you can do to improve your body language on television, it's to gesture with your hands. During the first round of interviews in my media training sessions, most people never move their hands. There's usually one of two reasons for this. The first is nerves. With a camera rolling, people often tense their bodies up and don't move anything. The other reason is because some ancient myth says you shouldn't move your hands because it'd shift the focus away from what you're saying. I've heard of some contemporary media and presentation trainers who still offer this advice.

Don't listen to them. You must gesture with your hands. You do it in everyday conversation, so why not for a media interview? This first reason you must do this is because it helps you come across as natural and genuine.

Next time you're watching a television news programme, look out for it. Those who gesture will look more credible than those who don't. Think of great the communicators of recent years, Bill Clinton, Tony Blair and Barack Obama. They all do it.

When you're watching the news, also listen to the voices of the guests. I bet the ones who aren't gesturing sound more monotone than those who do.

This is something that's not well known. The human communication system is all interlinked. When you gesture, your voice box is affected. It allows the tone of your voice to move up and down naturally, depending on the emphasis you place on specific words. This makes you sound interesting. In contrast, if you don't gesture, your voice is more monotone in nature. This not only makes you sound less convincing but it sounds boring to the audience. That means your messages are less likely to get through.

Gesturing also helps you relax. It gets rid of the nerves. That's because it feels more natural and the act of moving your hands helps you eliminate stress from the body.

Energy

A spokesperson without energy is like a comedian without jokes. Viewers get bored, they switch off and remember nothing of what was said. It also does nothing for the reputation of the spokesperson or the organisation he represents.

One problem with energy is the dumbing down effect that television or video has. What appears quite energetic at the time of the interview always looks less so when played back or seen by viewers watching at home.

If you fall into this category, you need to make a conscious effort to grow your intensity levels when facing a television interview. Don't go over the top, just increase your intensity to the maximum you're comfortable with. Marginally raising your voice can also grow your intensity.

The hand movement discussed above has a dramatic effect on energy. Once people start gesturing, their energy level usually increases greatly.

Move that head

Just as it's important to gesture with your hands, you also need to move your head. Once again, it's something we do in everyday life, so we should do it in media interviews. Nerves are the main reason some spokespeople keep their head still. Viewers watch your face closely to see your facial expressions. They do this as part of their assessment process. For example, if you're fronting a press conference after a disaster, they'll be watching your face to see if your expressions match your words. They'll be thinking things like, "Is she really remorseful or is she just saying that for the cameras?"

How do you come across? I've had media training clients who are horrified to realise they have irritating habits they never knew about. One man used to blink repeatedly while under pressure, while a female leader I trained used to flick her hair back every time she answered a question.

It's important to identify these habits and eliminate them. This comes with practice. The last thing you want is to find out about some irritating habit on live television in the midst of a crisis.

The more media interviews or practice sessions you do, the more competent you'll become. When that happens, the nerves will calm down and you'll be your natural self again. That's not to say there won't still be pressures.

Posture

When sitting for a television interview, it's important to have the correct posture. Some people slouch back in the chair and this not only looks unprofessional, it's difficult to gesture from that position. It also means the camera will focus on your stomach. It'll focus on whatever is closest to it.

Another group of spokespeople sit up as straight as they can in the chair. They appear to be tensing their muscles to stay in that spot. This makes them looks stiff and uncomfortable and it's also hard to gesture naturally in this position.

> # "What you do drowns out anything you say."
>
> ### 💬 Pete Burdon, 2015

The best way is to sit up straight but relaxed, with the upper part of your body facing slightly forward in the chair. Sit straight and then move your upper body forward about 15 degrees. This may seem uncomfortable to start with but it'll become natural. There are two reasons why it's important to do this. Firstly, by moving your body forward 15 degrees, the camera will focus on your face. Viewers are far more likely to hear and remember your messages if they're focused on where your words are coming from; your mouth, not your stomach.

Secondly, by sitting forward like this, you can place your hands comfortably on your upper legs. From there, gesturing with them is simple. In this position, men should have their legs about 30 centimetres apart and facing forward. Women are usually more comfortable crossing their legs. The best way to do this and not appear defensive is by crossing them at the ankles and angling them about 45 degrees to one side.

What about standing interviews?

Most of the principles applied to sitting interviews also relate to standing ones. It's still important to move your head and body and gesture with your hands. The only major difference is where to place your hands. It's easy to notice spokespeople who know what they're doing when you see how they stand during television interviews. Some stand with their hands behind their backs but this is the last place they should be. It not only looks awkward but it's impossible to gesture with them from there. That's one way to guarantee a monotone voice.

Some men clench their hands together over their private parts but this looks unnatural. The best way is to hold them somewhere either in front of your body or down beside your legs. You need to pick the spot that feels most natural. By all means, have one on top of the other if that's comfortable, just don't clench them together as that looks awkward and gives you less freedom to gesture.

Where should I look?

In almost every media interview situation, you need to look at the person asking the questions. If there are more people involved, look at the person who is talking. This shows that you're interested. Lots of people look away from the interviewer when they're answering questions. It's a natural thing to do, particularly when you're thinking about what to say, but you can't do this in a television interview. It can make you look uninterested or even untrustworthy. It's best to look at the person asking the questions pretty much all the time, then there's no risk of giving the wrong impression.

Satellite interviews

The only time you don't look at the person asking the question is during what's known as the 'down the line' or 'satellite' interview. This is where you're in one location and the interviewer is in a studio somewhere else. Here you need to look into a camera lens, rather than at a person. This is difficult for two major reasons. Firstly, it's hard to maintain your energy and passion while talking to a camera lens and secondly, you can't see what reaction your answers get from the interviewer or people in the studio.

You'll have seen hundreds of these interviews on television without realising it. They're the ones where there's a presenter or reporter interviewing someone who appears on a large screen in the studio. That person in the big screen is actually looking into a camera lens, not directly at the person asking the questions.

It's important to maintain eye contact with the camera lens throughout the interview. This is difficult. When you can't see your interviewer, it's hard not to look around at more interesting sights. This can include a small television monitor showing the interviewer in the studio on a slight delay. If you do that, you'll either look uninterested or untrustworthy. You'll literally look shifty-eyed. This is common. Next time you see an interview of this nature, look at the person in the big screen. I've often seen people look away, even when the interviewer is asking the question. If you're ever featuring in a satellite interview, make sure you keep your eyes on the lens throughout the interview, no matter how strange it feels. The last thing you want is for people to go away with a bad impression of you.

However, my advice is to avoid these interviews if at all possible. At times it may seem the most convenient option but if it's an important interview, you should seriously consider getting on a plane so you can be in the studio where the interviewer will be based. This is particularly vital if your opponents or competitors will be there. If you're not there under those circumstances, you're at a distinct disadvantage. You have little power to demand the floor or get as much attention as those sitting with the interviewer. You're at the mercy of the interviewer and show producer when it comes to how much attention you get. When they think you've finished expressing your point, they can cut you off immediately and that's when you're lucky enough to get your opportunity to speak. That doesn't happen if you are in the studio. I've seen this very thing happen recently in a by-election where the candidate from the governing party was almost totally shut out of the interview.

Body language for radio

You may think body language is irrelevant for radio, because there are no pictures but there's one reason that it's very important. I mentioned earlier how the body communicates as a system. Specifically, I mentioned how hand gestures affect the voice box and allow your voice tone to flow up and down, depending on the emphasis you place on specific words.

That's why it's so important that you still use these gestures when talking on radio. They give your voice that energy and passion and your tone of voice is the most important part of any radio interview. If you don't gesture like you must on television, you voice will sound monotone and boring. Next time you hear sound bites on a radio news bulletin, see how exciting they sound. Not the words but the tone of the voice expressing them. Most radio sound bites are monotone because most people giving radio interviews are doing so over the phone at their work desk. That means one hand is out of action because it's holding the phone in one ear and the other hand is often playing with a computer mouse or a pen scribbling notes. This means the hands aren't gesturing.

So what's the answer?

A headset solves this problem. To sound passionate on radio when giving the interview from work, you should walk around the room with your headset on. That way you'll express yourself far better than if you are sitting at a desk with a computer in front of you. When you find yourself in this position, try it out, then listen to yourself when the broadcast is aired. You'll be pleasantly surprised.

What about interviews with print reporters?

This is the type of interview when most spokespeople think there's no need to worry about body language. They're wrong again. It's true that it's not as important as it is for broadcasting interviews but it shouldn't be ignored. If you're doing a face to face interview with a print reporter, he'll be evaluating you throughout. This is where your body language is important. You want reporters to like you and know that you're an honest and trustworthy person. This becomes even more important if you come across that reporter again in a more serious situation. Perhaps your reputation could be on the line. If the reporter already trusts you and believes you're a good person, he's likely to go easier on you when the stakes are high.

There's another important reason why body language is important with print reporters. If the interview is for a more detailed piece, your body language could feature in the story. How many times have you read personal profiles where the mood of the interview subject becomes part of the story? I remember one a few years ago when a high-profile CEO was the focus of a report. It began something like, "He leant back with his arms folded." That automatically gave the impression he was defensive. If his body language was positive and he was full of enthusiasm, that may have been mentioned in the profile.

The bottom line is that body language is important in any media interview. In some situations it's more important but the best approach is to be positive around any journalist or presenter. In fact, this is important in other parts of your working life. That could include business meetings, job interviews or just day-to-day conversations with co-workers.

Body language when crisis strikes

When you face the media during a crisis, the stakes rise. We'll talk more about that later in the book but in these situations, whether they are emergencies or reputational issues, your body language will be under extra scrutiny.

The importance of this was uncovered by research undertaken in the 1960s by Professor Albert Mehrabian. It showed that when people are communicating feelings and attitudes, only seven percent of the message received comes from the words spoken. The tone of voice accounts for 38 percent, while a massive 55 percent of the message received comes from the body language.

This heavily raises the body language stakes when you have emotional news to announce. For example, if you ever need to announce the death of a staff member after some freak accident, people will be less interested in what you say, they'll focus on how you say it.

Body language and tone of voice are important in all media communications but clearly more so when your focus is of an emotional nature.

This is another reason why practice is so important. You may feel strong emotions if ever placed in a difficult position like the example above but with nerves and a lack of experience, it's easy to come across as cold and unfeeling.

What to wear

What should you wear on television? That all depends on the image you want to project. Who could forget Winston Churchill's pinstriped suits and cigar hanging out of his mouth? More recently, Barak Obama is always seen in a suit but often without the jacket. This is clearly designed to portray him more as one of the people, rather than their distant leader. Steve Jobs was different again. He wanted to project a more laid back style. He'd never wear a tie and often appeared in front of the media in jeans.

So what image do you want to portray? It's important to know this before your first television interview. In most cases this will mean dressing well without going over the top. This is of course, unless your image is to be eccentric.

There are things you must stay clear of. Checks, stripes and boxes look blurred on television. White can be bright and glary, although white shirts are still the favourite of Barak Obama. Businessmen are best with dark suits and a blue shirt. Always make sure your tie goes with the shirt.

Women are better with darker colours also. It's all about making people focus on your face and not drawing their eyes to your interesting clothing. If women wear a bright red dress or men wear a pink tie, the audience is more likely to focus on the clothing, rather than the message. Dangly jewellery is also a bad idea. Not only does it detract from the message but it can reflect off studio lights.

Always go with the best clothing for the time and place. A suit is usually good for professional men but if the interview is at your house on a Saturday evening beside the barbeque, this wouldn't work. In these situations, it's still important to look tidy without going over the top. In a nutshell, it's best to dress conservatively so people are totally focused on what you're saying.

What's changed in the digital age?

Body language has become more important in the digital age. Firstly, the new role of multimedia journalist means that more of your interviews will become multi-platform. In other words, just because you're doing an interview with a well-known newspaper company, don't assume the story will only appear in print. You may find the interview is recorded on video and placed on the company website. It could also be used as an audio only story.

This means that your body language will become just as important with print reporters. This is already happening, so remember to ask reporters exactly what formats they want to use when they interview you. Also remember that most radio networks now have webcams placed in studios so that audiences can watch the proceedings through the network website. Radio is no longer just about audio, which means you should carefully consider what you wear into the radio studio.

The growth in video technology is beginning to have a major impact on modern leaders. In her book, 'The Silent Language of Leaders' Carol Kinsey Goman predicts that the visual technology revolution will make body language skills even more critical than they are today.

She says videoconferencing that allows participants to see each other can help build stronger bonds and improve rapport.

> "Video communication can also heighten a participant's anxiety and self-consciousness because there is no hiding behind a text message or computer screen."
>
> 💬 **Carol Kinsey Goman,**
> *The Silent Language of Leaders,* 2011.

This shows that body language is not only becoming more important in the modern era when it comes to media interviews, it's also something that today's leaders will be increasingly judged on in their everyday roles.

Answering Questions

CHAPTER SIX

Answering Questions

When preparing for a media interview, lots of people brainstorm for hours to try and predict every possible question they could be asked. That's not necessary because you can never be 100 percent sure of what they will ask. The important thing to remember is that you have 100 percent control of what comes out of your mouth.

> # "It's not the questions that damage you, but how you respond to them."
>
> ## 🗨 Pete Burdon, 2015

The reporter picks the topic and the questions and you decide what your responses will be. That isn't to say that you shouldn't give thought as to what will be asked. A good way to do this is to use the questioning system that journalism schools tell their students to use. This is the old five Ws and the H. They're told to focus their questions around, Where? When? Why? What? Who? and How? So have a quick think about what questions you could be asked that begin with these words. This will quickly uncover 99 percent of the difficult ones that require more preparation.

For example, let's say you're a government minister responsible for corrections when it's decided to build a new prison to take pressure off overcrowding. The big question people will want to know is, "Where will the prison be built?" There will be many other questions but that'd probably be the focus the journalist would chose to base the story on.

What about a suspicious fire at your workplace? Again, there would be many questions asked. In this case, 'how' questions could dominate i.e. 'How many people were injured or killed?' and 'How could this happen?' and 'How did the fire start?'

Creating your media message and sound bites should be your focus but you should also have a good idea of what the reporter is likely to ask you. Conducting this exercise will help you identify this quickly. It'll also help you identify the difficult questions that you may need time to organise responses for.

Context

Most people think that media interviews are simple, reporters ask questions and you answer them, but it's not that simple with the media. It's all because journalists can pull quotes out of context.

A quote by its very definition is pulled out of context. This is difficult for many because throughout our life we've answered questions by starting at the beginning and giving lengthy responses, while being able to reference back to earlier points. That isn't possible in media interviews.

You could talk to a journalist for an hour or 10 hours and she may pluck a 10 second quote from the entire interview and use that as the focus of the story. That's why everything you say must be able to stand on its own and not be reliant on other answers or other parts of lengthy responses.

This is different from any other conversation you'll ever encounter.

It requires practice to master. It means you must avoid the temptation to answer in detail. If you do, only a part of that answer will appear in the story and the reporter will decide what part that is.

I must make something clear at the outset. I'm not telling you to avoid answering questions. If you do, you'll irritate the reporter and you'll also lose credibility amongst your audience if it's a live interview.

You should always answer the question but don't spend too long before transferring back to one of your key points. We'll focus on how to do that shortly.

Former British Labour Party leader, Ed Miliband, found this out the hard way. In 2011, he was interviewed about public sector strikes. His response to the first question was, "These strikes are wrong at a time when negotiations are still going on but parents and the public are being let down by both sides because the government has acted in a reckless and provocative manner. I urge both sides to put aside the rhetoric, get around the negotiating table and stop this from happening again."

That sounds like a reasonable answer. The problem was that Miliband repeated the same words almost verbatim when answering the following four questions.

His repetitive answer and failure to answer the questions became the story itself. The reporter said after the interview that he was ashamed of the political discourtesy he was shown in being used as a recording device for a scripted sound bite. The story was brought up again during the British general election of 2015. A video of the interview on YouTube was watched 1.3 million times over a five day period.

This is why you should always answer the question. But don't answer in too much detail before returning to a key point or a sound bite based on a key point.

The art of bridging

Bridging is an important element in media interviews. It's the transitional statement you use to move back to a key point after you've answered a question. Bridging should be done throughout an interview. It's how you influence what parts of taped broadcast interviews and all print interviews make it into the final story. The other option is to merely answer questions. That leaves all the power over what's used to the reporter.

Some people call this spin, but that's unfair. We've already covered how important it is that your key points be of interest to the audience of the reporter. We've also covered how to present those points in attractive ways to help the reporter produce an interesting story.

So if we answer the questions asked of us, plus add our own relevant and interesting points to the conversation, everyone wins. We get our points across and the reporter gets a good story.

For example, if there was a fire at your workplace, a reporter may ask you when you had your last fire drill. You could say, "We had a fire drill last week" but rather than stop there, you could use a bridging statement such as, "Let me just add that," as a bridging statement, before tagging on a key point like, "We'll be launching an investigation into what caused the fire and how we can improve our evacuation procedures."

In that example, we've answered the question and managed to slot in one of our key points.

This works just as well in more positive interviews. Let's say your business has just won the Business of the Year Award. A reporter may ask you how you feel about winning the award and you may answer, "I feel so proud of myself for winning this." Once again, you could then use a bridging statement such as, "But what's more important is," before coming back to a key point, "It will allow me to give far more back to the community where I grew up." That's assuming that this statement was one of your key points.

At another stage of the interview, you may want to bridge back to the same point but this time you may use an example of what you'll now be able to give back. As we covered when focusing on sound bites, reporters love using examples in their stories. It makes an abstract point concrete and gives you another way to get the point across. You'll also avoid sounding like a broken record as Ed Miliband did.

Here's another example of how that could play out. The reporter may ask you later in the interview what you believe made you a successful entrepreneur. You could answer with, "I think hard work is the only way to get ahead in life," but then bridge with a statement like, "But what really excites me about winning this award is that," then add the sound bite, "This will allow me to upgrade the local cricket pavilion where I played as a teenager."

One again, you get the point across that it'll allow you to give back to the community but this time with an example, rather than the key point itself.

Bridging techniques are your key to getting your points across but always remember to answer the question first. Here are a few other bridging techniques you've probably seen used before.

- The real issue here is
- Looking at the big picture
- At the end of the day, what this means is
- Building on that point
- The bigger point here is

There are literally hundreds of these to choose from and you need to use the ones you're most comfortable with but never use the same one all the time. This can seem like you're repeating your answer, even though you're not.

Know your target

While bridging is vital, there are other things to remember when answering questions. Firstly, you need to know who you're talking to. Your target is the person reading the newspaper or watching the television news, it's not the reporter or presenter asking the questions.

Many spokespeople fall into this trap. They think they have to please the reporter all the time. As we've discussed, we'll do all we can to help the reporter because that's our best approach to get an accurate and positive story written or broadcast but it won't always be possible.

For example, if you're in the midst of a serious crisis, there will be things you can't tell a reporter. This is usually because you don't know the answer but the reporter needs a good story so will push you for information. That's her job but it doesn't mean you have to give away information you either don't know or can't reveal.

If it's a live interview, people watching or listening will make up their own mind about how reasonable you're being. If the journalist takes exception to you holding back information, the audience will make up their own minds about whether you should reveal it or not. They're the ones you need to convince, not the person asking the questions.

Remember that live interviews are an opportunity for you to impress the audience and the reporter or presenter is your vehicle to get those messages through. They're not your target.

Having said that, think carefully before withholding information. There will be good reasons at times but sometimes people refuse to share information when it wouldn't do them any harm. Always think, "What's the worst thing that can happen if I say this?" If your answer isn't as bad as you thought, release it. It'll help your relationship with the media and highlight your willingness to cooperate when you can.

When you do need to withhold things, it's important to say why. It could be because something is before the courts and you aren't legally allowed to reveal it or you may decide not to reveal someone's name because you believe they deserve privacy. Once again, say so. Reporters are more concerned when you don't give a reason. They also become suspicious and will do all they can to find out through other means.

So while you should do all you can to help reporters, remember they aren't your target audience.

Keep it simple

Newspapers are written so that 11-year-olds can understand the language. That's not because they're written for 11-year-olds or that readers are stupid, it's because simple language is easier for everyone to read, understand and remember.

Even if sophisticated readers are the target audience, it still makes sense to use simple language. Let's look at two ways of saying the same thing.

Version One: It was significantly advantageous for our company to take ownership of the recent bullying issues, despite our rigorous policies and procedures in this area.

Version Two: The best thing we could do was review our bullying policies.

While we understand both versions, it takes us longer to register version one. It's also unlikely to stick with us as long as version two because of the more difficult language used.

I've already mentioned the importance of using basic language in your media messages. The same applies to the rest of your answers. There's another problem with using more sophisticated language and this is more important with broadcasting interviews. When it takes us longer to register a point, we're often not listening to the point that follows it but when the language is simple, we understand and remember it without even having to think about what it means.

Jargon is important to keep in mind when facing the media. We all have our own professions and these have their own distinct jargon. It's easy to assume everyone understand this when many have no idea. For example, I do lots of training in the educational sector, some of which involves school principals. In my media interview sessions, they often talk about restorative justice as an important element in resolving issues regarding bullying. This is a term they understand because it's a common term among primary and secondary educationalists but someone who has no knowledge of this sector wouldn't understand what it means. So rather than talk about restorative justice, they need to break the term down to something more understandable and concrete.

Think about your industry. What terms do you use that you may wrongly assume people understand? I've fallen into this trap myself. For the last two decades, I've assumed that everyone knows what a press release is but a few years ago I was asked by a company CEO what the term meant. This surprised me at first but when I thought about it, I realised that if someone had never had contact with the news media or public relations industry, how would they know?

If you use jargon in a media interview, the person asking the questions will often ask you to explain but this won't always happen, particularly if the journalist is a specialist in your area. They can fall into the same trap so never take jargon for granted. If in doubt, spell it out.

Detail is your enemy

Always avoid the temptation to answer in detail. It's tempting to try to impress the reporter with your knowledge and go into major detail. This doesn't work in the media. It'll only get you into trouble or prevent you from getting your key points through the editing process. Remember that unless your interview is for live broadcast, only snippets of what you say will end up in the subsequent story.

How many times have you heard someone say they were quoted out of context? Most of the time this is because the interviewee talks too much. You should answer the question, bridge to a key point and then shut your mouth. This does vary slightly for different interview types and these will be discussed shortly but even for extended print interviews, you must be careful not to say too much.

One famous example of this was the Richard Nixon Watergate speech mentioned earlier. While this was not a media interview, the principle is the same and the media were there to report on the speech. The vast majority of what Nixon said would have looked good on television news or in a newspaper if that had been what reporters chose to select for their stories but he continued on after making these positive points. He ended by saying, "People need to know if their President's a crook. Well, I'm not a crook. I've earned everything I've got."

As you'll be aware, the part of that speech that became famous was when he said, "I'm not a crook." That's been used in media all over the world ever since.

Was it taken out of context? Possibly. Did he say those words? Yes. The key is not to say anything you don't want to see in the subsequent story. That's the only way to make sure it isn't used. In other words, everything is fair game. This takes discipline and practice but it can be mastered.

> "It is always a risk to speak to the press; they are likely to report what you say."
>
> 💬 **Hubert H. Humphrey**

What people say is often taken out of context. I've had numerous clients come to my media training sessions after they've had a bad experience with the media. They claim their words were taken out of context and sometimes they have a point. The meaning of what you say can be manipulated. For example, if you were asked by a journalist if you have a crisis communication plan, you could respond with, "We don't have a crisis communication plan but we've just hired a public relations company to develop one for us. It'll be in place next month."

The reporter could select the first part of your answer and focus the story on the fact that you don't have a plan. You could justifiably argue that it was taken out of context however, you still said you don't have one. The best way to answer this question would be to omit the first part and focus on the second, then you're only using positive language and avoiding the risk of the journalist using the first part alone.

What if you don't know the answer?

It's normally perfectly reasonable to admit that you don't know the answer to a question. It's far better to do this than give an answer you're unsure about because you'll not only be seen as incompetent when someone reveals you were wrong but you'll also seem untrustworthy. This is the last thing a leader from any sector needs. If you don't know the answer to a question, say so. You can offer to get the answer later. The only stipulation is that you follow through with that promise. If you don't, you'll harm any relationship you've developed with the person asking the questions.

If it's something you believe you should know and it may be seen as incompetent if you don't answer, there's one technique you can try. You can bridge away with a statement such as, "I don't know that but what I do know is" or you could say, "That's unclear but what is clear is." Then you follow up with a key point or a sound bite.

The need to avoid incorrect answers rises steeply in a crisis. In many situations, you won't be expected to know so you'll need to use statements like, "We don't have that information yet but we'll let you know as soon as we have more." I'll focus more on dealing with the media in a crisis later in the book.

Empathy when answering questions

We discussed the importance of using empathy as a key point when your media interview is focused on a crisis with a victim. In some interviews, you could get a specific question that requires empathy in your answer, even if it's not one of your key points. For example, you could be a politician midway through an interview focused on your government's new minimum wage policy and your media message may centre totally on the benefits of the policy. However you could get a question from the reporter about a business owner who'd made an employee redundant because he couldn't afford to pay every worker the new wage. You would still want to focus on your message but should still empathise with the redundant worker as part of your answer.

Just a simple statement like, "I sympathise with that worker," before returning to a key point would be all you need to do. If you don't empathise with the worker, you may come across as heartless.

What's changed in the digital age?

The ability to answer questions and bridge back to key points successfully has always been a difficult task for spokespeople but it's never been more important than it is today. With so little time to make your point, the ability to make the most of your time in the spotlight is vital. It'll be a major determinant in your success as a leader and this isn't only in media interviews, it's in all areas of business. With so many messages competing for the limelight and so little time to present your points, you must make every second count when addressing stakeholders through any medium.

Answering questions will become even more of an art form as the digital age continues to transform communication. George Bernard Shaw's quote that, "Communication only occurs when your message registers with the intended recipient," couldn't be more relevant.

Adapting to different interview formats

CHAPTER SEVEN

Adapting to different interview formats

While the vast majority of this book covers print and broadcast media as one, there are subtle differences that you must be aware of.

Print media

Print reporters have more space to fill with their stories, so you can expect more questions to be asked of you. The extent of this will depend on whether you are being interviewed for a news story or a detailed feature. This is something you need to find out when you're first approached.

If it's a news story for a newspaper, the reporter is will be looking for a few direct quotes and background information. If it's a feature, you can expect a longer interview.

In both situations, the reporter will want more than her broadcasting counterparts but be careful, print interviews are more dangerous than any other.

Some people think they can go into major detail with print. Clearly, you can say more, but not too much more. As I've said earlier, the more you say, the more you give control back to the reporter to decide what's used in the subsequent story. You're still best to answer the question briefly before transferring back to a key point or prepared sound bite, then be quiet, otherwise you lower the chance of your key points making it into the story or worse, your words are taken out of context. Complaints about spokespeople being quoted out of context are far more common in print media.

If it's a longer feature, some trainers will suggest you use more than three key points. This is the wrong advice as it only reduces the chances of you getting your points into the story. Even feature stories only use a few main points. You'd be surprised at how many column centimetres your media message, sound bites, background and answers to questions can take up.

I'm certainly not telling you to blindly avoid questions, you should answer them, and in a feature story, you'll be asked more. For example, if it's a feature profiling you, you can expect many personal questions. You may be asked about your childhood, work background and family circumstances. Your answers to these questions will take up space but you should still have a focus on bridging back to your media message.

The best advice with features is to prepare more direct quotes for your points. This way you can give more relevant and interesting quotes to the reporter, while also answering his questions. Don't be fooled by a print interview. You must still be focused and avoid answering in too much detail.

Another reason for this is something that distinguishes print media from any other form. You can't talk to the audience directly. Unlike live broadcast interviews, you must rely on the reporter to tell your story for you. That's why it's so important to have gripping quotes that will be used verbatim. That way, you have more control over what's used. This is also why you must be incredibly clear with your answers and messages.

The last thing you want is to be misquoted. The more detail you use and the more sophisticated your language, the more likely this becomes.

Something else to bear in mind with newspapers is the role of the sub-editor. You may not be aware that once a reporter has written the story, it's sent to a sub-editor. That person comes up with the headline and edits the story further so that it fits nicely into the space provided for it on the page.

If the story is unclear or boring, the sub-editor may make changes that alter the context or meaning of it. This happens particularly when the story is written by a junior reporter. It happened to me in my first role as a journalist. The headline made the story look worse than I'd intended but that was my fault, not the sub-editor's. That's because my first paragraph didn't clearly sum up the story. It should always do this. The sub-editor took a different meaning from that first paragraph and that was reflected in the negative headline.

If the person I was interviewing had been clearer, more interesting and briefer, I would've written a clearer first paragraph and story. I'm not trying to pass the buck in this situation, this was clearly my fault, but when a reporter's on a tight deadline, you can understand how this can happen. To avoid this as a spokesperson, be clear, interesting and brief.

There's another important technique that you can use to minimise your risk of being misquoted or taken out of context by print reporters. That's the speed at which you talk. If you're sitting down with the reporter, keep an eye on how quickly he's taking notes. If he can't keep up with you, he'll either miss important information or get it wrong. This was a common problem I faced as a reporter. I'd sometimes have to write so fast that I couldn't understand my notes when it came to writing the story. This put me under pressure when a deadline was looming. There are two possible outcomes when this happens; you're misquoted or you're left out of the story.

Some reporters these days take notes on a PC instead of using a notebook and pen. This will make it easier for you to notice if you're talking too quickly. If the reporter is typing furiously on her keyboard, you need to slow down. You should also listen for this when it's a telephone interview.

Another thing to remember with print interviews is the potential for a photographer to accompany the reporter to an interview. This can happen whether the interview is at your premises or at the media outlet. If it's a telephone interview, the reporter may arrange for a photographer to meet you later.

If you're meeting the reporter in person, you can either find out in advance whether a photo will be taken or assume it will happen. Make sure you're appropriately dressed for the message you want to send and consider the backdrop to the photograph. If it's a positive story and the photo will be taken at your premises, suggest a favourable location such as in front of your colourful organisation sign. You could also give the photographer some ideas that will fit in with the context of the story. For example, if the story's about a new clean water filter your business has just developed, you could suggest the photograph shows you filling a fresh glass of water from the filter.

While it's good to make suggestions, remember that photographers are professionals and know what a good photo looks like. They make the final decision.

The only exception to this is if you think their idea could cause you some embarrassment. This is unlikely but worth bearing in mind. For example, if you're a business owner discussing the risk of drink driving after work drinks, make sure there are no bottles of wine clearly visible behind you.

Broadcast Interviews

Whether its radio or television, broadcast interviews fall into two basic categories. The first is where a reporter will be looking for one or two sound bites to form part of a story for a news bulletin and the second is a live interview where you're talking directly to a reporter or presenter in real time. The only exception to this is the pre-recorded interview that's presented verbatim at a later date.

So what are the differences? Firstly, where the interview is for a news story only, the needs of the reporter are quite different. Due to the brevity of broadcast news stories, all she'll want from you is a short sound bite or two. Time won't allow for any more. This is why you must focus on giving good sound bites that last a matter of seconds. These days they commonly only last seven seconds but in extreme cases can be up to 15. You should keep them under 10 seconds and use the techniques outlined earlier to construct them.

If you can't sum up your point in an interesting way in 10 seconds or less, you'll not only risk being misquoted but you'll have done the reporter a disservice. This leads to one of two possibilities. The first is that she only uses a part of what you said, which may cause context problems. In other words, it may not make sense without the rest of your point to provide the necessary context. The second option is for her to paraphrase what you said. This limits her ability to bring the story to life with an exciting sound bite and it increases the chance of her missing the point you were trying to make altogether. When this happens, everyone loses.

There are no other media interview type that demands more rigorous discipline. Answer the question as briefly as possible, then bridge to a point or sound bite. There will be times when you can almost bridge immediately. Then stop talking. Even if there's silence, stop talking. Silence is the responsibility of the interviewer to fill. One tactic that makes this easier is to pause before you answer. You're quite entitled to pause for a few seconds. This gives you time to think about what to say. The reporter will be quite happy for you to pause as not only will it give her better material to use but pauses help in the editing process when it comes to selecting what parts of the interview to use as sound bites.

There's another vital element in broadcasting interviews for news bulletins. Because time is so short, viewers won't hear the questions asked of you which means that your answers need to incorporate the question to make what you said quotable. For example, if you were asked what your number one priority was after a major accident, you might say, "Supporting the victims," but that can't be used as a direct sound bite because people have no idea of the context of that statement. So you're best off saying, "Our number one priority now is supporting the victims." You can see how that incorporates the question and answers it in the same brief sentence.

Your key points and sound bites should speak for themselves and incorporate the context in an interview. If they don't, they're not good enough to be used.

Live Broadcast interviews

In many ways, live broadcast interviews are the safer option. This is particularly so when it comes to high stakes topics. I discussed earlier how this is a way to eliminate the chances of your words being taken out of context.

Another reason they can be a safe option is that viewers or listeners get a better gauge of you as a person. If your interviewer's tough on you, audience members will make up their own mind about how effective or credible you are. While regulars tuning in to these interviews often develop a bond with the presenter, they also realise when that person goes too far. If you remain calm in the face of an aggressive interviewer, you'll come out on top in the eyes of viewers or listeners.

This is in stark contrast to an aggressive interviewer putting together a news story. That person could be highly aggressive and rude while asking you questions which could lead you to lose your cool. The problem in this scenario is that people won't see or hear the reporter asking the questions, they'll only see your answers. Then they will have a totally different opinion of you without seeing the barrage you had to put up with.

The credibility issue works both ways in live interviews. It's more important to answer the questions in live interviews than in any other context. If you clearly dodge a question, the audience will see it as clearly as the person asking the question will. This can dent your reputation severely. There will be times when you can't answer a question and we'll deal with that in a later chapter but unless there's some undeniable reason not to, you must answer the question in some way.

One thing you don't need to do in a live interview is incorporate the questions into your answers because people will see or hear the questions as clearly as you will. Another major difference is when it comes to pausing. These are a great idea in news story interviews but not live ones. If there's one thing the broadcasting media despise, its silence or 'dead air,' as it's often referred to. You must respond to questions almost immediately.

As in all the other interview formats discussed above, you still need to focus on bridging back to key message points and sound bites. Although there's usually more time in a live interview, you still need to narrow your focus to three key points. Keep in mind that people only ever remember a few things from an interview. You want those things to be the points you selected. Also be aware that snippets of the live interview will probably be used in later news bulletins. That gives you another opportunity to get your points across.

What's changed in the digital age?

Skype interviews

Media interviews through Skype and other similar platforms are becoming more prominent in the digital age. Most of the techniques for other formats should be followed on Skype but there are some unique differences.

Firstly, when a television crew comes to your office for an interview, they control sound, lighting and background but with Skype, you're the crew. If you're a former television cameraperson or an online video expert, you'll be more than qualified to deal with this but I'm assuming you don't fall into this category.

Lighting is vital in any visual interview and Skype is no different. The key here is having light projecting onto your face. So often you see an interview where the spokesperson looks dark compared to the background lighting. Place lights on both sides of your computer which are focused on you.

Sound is just as important. Make sure you're in a quiet room. There'll preferably be carpet on the ground to avoid echoing. The other issue with sound is the quality of your microphone. The built in one on your computer may be good enough but if you often use Skype for media interviews, it'd pay to invest in a higher quality mic to override your existing one.

Background is something many spokespeople forget about with Skype. This is another area where you're in control. The last thing you want is a messy office for all to see. Not only will it give a bad impression of you, it'll distract viewers away from what you're saying. A clear background can work but there's also an opportunity for you to place your organisation logo strategically behind you. Just make sure it won't be a distraction.

Body language is an area where Skype interviews need to be approached slightly differently. The first thing you need to do is raise your computer to eye level. How many Skype interviews have you seen where the spokesperson is looking down? The next thing is where to look. It's natural to look at the other person talking but people want you to be focused directly at them which is why you need to look into the webcam. If you don't, it'll appear that you're looking below them.

The big difference with body language between Skype and television is body movement. Depending on your bandwidth, your movements can look staggered and in separate frames, rather than in real time like television. This is why you may need to limit your movement on Skype, particularly hand gestures.

As we've already discussed, this can limit the impact of your performance. There are two ways to address this. Firstly, a permanent broadband connection will allow you to maximise the speed of your internet and secondly, you need to practice your interview with a colleague or friend shortly before the real thing. This way you'll see how well your connection is performing and how natural your body movements appear.

The need for practice isn't limited to determining your broadband speed. It's the only way to see how well you perform on Skype and it'll also test your lighting, sound and background. Some spokespeople don't take Skype interviews as seriously as television because it doesn't seem as real but remember, there are just as many people watching and your reputation is still on the line.

Interview
landmines
to avoid

CHAPTER EIGHT

Interview landmines to avoid

Yes or No demands

In negative situations, you may be asked by a reporter to give a 'yes' or 'no' answer. In some situations, there's no problem with this but in others, you can get yourself into trouble by giving such a black or white answer.

For example, if a worker had been killed in a factory accident, you could be asked, "Could another worker suffer a similar fate, yes or no?" You can't say no because it's always a possibility, regardless of how unlikely, but if you say yes, you could be in even more trouble.

This is where a media interview is different from any other conversation. You may believe the best answer is, "Yes, it's possible we will have another similar accident but our safety precautions are among the best in the world and the chances of a repeat are almost impossible."

In any other context, that would be a perfectly reasonable answer. The problem is that you have no idea what part of that answer will make it into an edited story. It's possible that the headline could read something like, "Factory boss admits another fatality could be just around the corner" with the second part of your answer being totally ignored.

What about the alternative? If you said no, your answer would lack credibility. Your audience would know that's untrue and you could also be accused of failing to take the issue seriously.

The best way to deal with these situations is to create your own answer and say something like, "Safety is our top priority and the precautions we take are among the best in the world." If that doesn't satisfy the reporter and he asks you again, you just have to repeat the answer. If you're asked a third time, you need to say something like, "I believe I've answered your question."

Another common question is to be asked for a guarantee. In this same example, the reporter may ask you, "Can you guarantee this won't happen again?" You clearly can't guarantee that but in this situation, you can use the word 'guarantee' in your answer. You could say, "What I can guarantee is that safety is our top priority and our precautions are among the best in the world."

Bear in mind that most reporters won't go for this sensationalism but some will and there are lots of cases where this has happened. You'll see an example in the chapter on crisis communication.

Always remember to bridge back to your key points after tough questions like this. It's easy to forget about them when you're under the pump but they are the points you want to get across in your interview. It's also the best tactic to get the interviewer away from a dangerous area and back to safer ground.

Never use negative language

Many spokespeople, whether in high profile positions or novices, fall into the trap of using negative language. I mentioned earlier how journalists producing news stories need you to answer in complete sentences. There's one exception to this and it's an important one.

Never repeat negative language, always choose a positive alternative. For example, let's say you're the CEO of a company in the middle of a major strike by your workers. A reporter could say to you, "You have terrible workplace relations policies, don't you?"

Your natural reaction would be to start your response with, "We don't have terrible workplace relations policies." The problem with that is you've just given the reporter an exciting negative quote to base his entire story on. That statement could be used as the headline of the story or as the story's major quote or sound bite.

It'll then be negative towards you and based on your denial. If you used a positive statement in response, the story could become positive. You could have responded with, "The benefits we give our staff are well above industry standards and we're proud of how we deal with staff." You can see how much more positive that sounds, while also answering the question. Instead of a negative denial, you're saying something positive about your business.

There are famous examples from history where experienced leaders used negative language that's worked against them. Richard Nixon's "I'm not a crook," is the best example, closely followed by Bill Clinton's, "I did not have sexual relations with that woman." Don't fall into the same trap.

Don't speculate

Reporters will always ask spokespeople to speculate. They're just doing their job and there will be times when speculation is quite appropriate. For example, the local reporter might ask you what you think the score will be in the World Cup Final. Giving your view is unlikely to harm anyone, unless such an answer could create political implications.

However, in more serious circumstances, it's best not to get drawn into the speculation game. This is particularly so when it's a negative issue. For example, let's say you're a big employer in a small town during an economic recession and you've already said redundancies are possible. A reporter asks you, "If redundancies do come, who'll be the first workers to go?" Until you know exactly what will happen and exactly who'll lose their jobs, you'd be asking for trouble by answering that question. Imagine the headlines in the following day's newspaper. Your answer would be sensationalised. You'd also see reporters visit those workers who you'd mentioned. Your best way to deal with this is to bridge away and go back to a key point. For example, you could say something like, "That'd be mere speculation. Our focus is on surviving the economic downturn so we can keep everyone employed."

Once you've decided who'll be made redundant and you've broken the news to those workers, you're best to inform the media quickly.

Face up to loaded questions

Loaded questions include an assumption. For example, a reporter may ask, "Since your business has an issue with employing women, don't you think you should change your policy towards gender equality?" Clearly, the reporter has asked that question on the assumption that it's common knowledge that your business doesn't like employing women.

If you fail to dispute the first part of that question and only respond to the second, you've just agreed with the assumption. Whatever the type of interview, you must challenge incorrect assumptions. You could say, "I dispute the premise of the question. We welcome female employees into our business" and remember not to use negative language. The most obvious answer would be, "We don't have an issue with employing women" which would be fine in any other context but not a media interview.

If the interviewer goes off topic

You've prepared your media message, accompanying sound bites and the interview's going well when suddenly the reporter asks you a question totally unrelated to the topic you agreed to talk about. What do you do? The answer to this depends on whether it's something that's just happened and you couldn't be expected to know more in which case it's quite acceptable to say you'll need to see the details before you can comment. Say that you are happy to get back to the reporter and make sure you do.

If the new question is about something commonly known, you should offer a brief comment followed by a bridge back to one of your key points. For example, let's say you're the leader of a political party and your interview is about your party's push for a higher minimum wage. Then the reporter asks you about recent criticism of your party's support of same sex marriage. For example, "Why does your party support same sex marriage?" You could answer, "We believe everyone should be equal before the law but what I'm here to talk to you about is the need for us to support those workers who are still living in poverty."

What's your personal opinion?

Reporters in today's world love using emotion in their stories. You often see presenters ask reporters at the scene of a disaster how the event has affected them personally. They'll first ask about the latest information on the disaster, then they often ask about the emotional impact it had on the reporter.

This is a major change in journalism. Reporters have traditionally been strictly suppliers of fact and other people's opinions. Their personal feelings have been irrelevant.

This concept of personal opinions and feeling has now shifted to official spokespeople. If you speak for a specific organisation, you're used to answering media questions based on your professional position but now some reporters have begun a trend in asking about your personal opinion. For example, let's say you're a spokesperson for the tobacco industry. A reporter challenges you about your industry's failure to recognise the safety risk of smoking. As spokesperson, you may reply that the industry has recognised the safety risks and has a number of programmes in place to address these. You may then mention a few examples.

But then the reporter may ask if you personally think the industry is doing enough to stop young people taking up the habit. If you don't, you may be tempted to say that you think more needs to be done. You then say that it's your personal opinion and doesn't represent the views of the industry.

As I'm sure you're aware, that won't work. You'll have just given the reporter a fantastic story angle. The headline would read something like, "Tobacco industry spokesperson at odds with policy."

You can't distinguish between your opinion and that of your employer. So how should you respond? You simply say you're speaking on behalf of your industry and bridge to another key point. If pushed, you need to repeat your answer.

If you feel uncomfortable doing this because you have a differing opinion, you need to decide whether the job is suitable for you.

What's changed in the digital age?

The risk of falling into these traps has grown in the digital age because organisations and individuals have so many communication platforms. While you should avoid using negative language in media interviews, it's also sensible to avoid it when posting to social media or on your website. The media have access to all of this information and they are quite entitled to quote you from these sources.

The same goes for your personal opinion. Keep any disagreement you have with your employer to yourself or at least off social media otherwise you may find it on the front page of your local newspaper.

Post Interview do's and don'ts

CHAPTER NINE

Post Interview do's and don'ts

Some spokespeople make the fatal mistake of assuming the interview is over when the camera's switched off or the print reporter stops taking notes. Your interview begins the second you make contact and doesn't end until you part ways.

If it's a broadcast interview, there'll be time to have a brief chat to the reporter or presenter before recording begins. This is a good time to exchange pleasantries but be aware that anything you say could be mentioned in the interview or subsequent story. Don't think information from this discussion is off limits. Everything is fair game. The same applies when recording ends.

If you fall into this trap, you won' be the first or the last. While this may seem obvious, a number of public figures have learnt this lesson the hard way. Political leaders are not exempt from the list. Former New Zealand and British Prime Ministers were caught doing this while leading their respective counties. However, their mistakes pale in comparison with former US President Ronald Reagan. During a sound check before a regular radio address in 1984, he said, "My fellow Americans, I'm pleased to tell you today that I've signed legislation that will outlaw Russia forever. We begin bombing in five minutes." While that wasn't broadcast, it was leaked to the public. It was later reported that the Soviet Far East Army was placed on alert after word of the statement got out.

Remember this story both before and after your 'official interview,' whether it's for print or broadcast media.

Don't ask to see a copy

When I was a daily news reporter, I occasionally had sources ask to see a copy of my story before I submitted it. The validity of requesting this is a common question I get in my media training workshops.

The answer is a simple 'don't ask.' Most media outlets have a policy that doesn't allow this. It's also highly insulting to the reporter. I once told my editor about such a request I had and his response was to tell the source to take out an advertisement if he wanted to dictate the content of a story.

I understand the reason for asking. You're concerned about being misquoted or your words being taken out of context. This is a valid worry but the best way to avoid that possibility is to follow the advice in this book. Create simple and brief messages to get across and answer questions briefly using clear language. If you do that, you shouldn't have any problems. Trouble usually occurs when spokespeople go into too much detail, don't have clear messages and use jargon from their industry. They then wonder why a particular segment of their interview becomes the focus of the story.

There's something else you can do. You can tell the reporter you are available to check any facts or quotes if she wants to clarify anything. That's far more professional and it'll also be appreciated by the reporter.

Contact those who didn't appear

If you hold a press conference or another event where you invite the media, some reporters won't show up even if they said they will. This happened to me while I was working as a communication manager for a major lobby group. I'd organised an event where local members of parliament were invited to go for a ride with a trucking operator from their constituency. Following the one hour drive, they were to meet at a specific spot for morning tea and a chat with the media and a national television network had agreed to come to the event. However, when they didn't arrive, I contacted them to hear they'd been diverted to a double murder. The first thing I did was send information about the event in the form of a press statement to that network. They then ran a brief story about it on the evening news.

A story would never have run on that network if I hadn't sent that information through. You, or the person responsible for your public relations, should do the same for anyone who fails to appear at your events. This is particularly so if they said they'd be there. Chances are that something deemed more important came up. This is common. You can sometimes salvage it by following up with useful information. This should apply whether the topic of your event is positive or negative. Remember that it's vital that your points are aired in any story that may portray you in a bad light.

Post Interview Footage

With television, the crew may want to record footage of you talking to the reporter once the interview has concluded. The words won't be used but it gives editors different camera angles to use when they put the interview package together for broadcast. You'll have seen this many times. Instead of seeing the interview subjects from the same head-on cameras the entire time, you occasionally see it from side on or from a different angle. This makes the story more interesting. If it's a serious topic you've just discussed, never laugh or smile when this footage is being taken because it'll be edited into the interview segment and appear as if you were laughing during the interview. This is important to remember because when this post interview process happens, you'll probably be sensing a sigh of relief and relaxing to the point of smiling loudly or even laughing.

What's changed in the digital age?

The need for speed has added pressure to the spokesperson in the digital age but there's one benefit to this change. It means that stories, particularly those in the print media, often appear on websites shortly after they've been written. This means that you can keep an eye out for them. If you do notice a serious mistake, you or a public relations employee can contact the reporter immediately. If she agrees with your concerns, the story can be quickly corrected. Then when it appears in the print publication, it'll be accurate. Before the advent of the internet, you had to wait for the newspaper to be published before you saw the story and by then it was too late for a correction. Always keep an eye on the website of the media outlet you were interviewed by. This is particularly important if the stakes are high. The story won't always appear on the website before the print publication is distributed but it will in many cases.

CHAPTER TEN

When crisis
strikes

CHAPTER TEN

When crisis strikes

The phone rings. It's a police officer telling you that a bus carrying 10 of your staff home from a corporate retreat has crashed. All 10 staff are in a serious condition and they've been flown to the nearest hospital.

Five minutes later a television reporter rings wanting an interview with you about the crash. She tells you a television crew is on its way to your office. Next, you hear that a picture of the bus is on Facebook. Then family members of the staff on the bus start arriving at your office. Crises like this are possible in any organisation. They come in all shapes and sizes.

What's your role as leader?

Your role in a crisis like this is vital. Your attitude towards crisis communication will largely determine the fate of your organisation if the unthinkable happens. The first thing you need to do is make sure you have a modern crisis communication plan in place. It's too late to deal with situations like this when they happen. Most organisations have evacuation plans, possibly business continuity plans or even emergency management plans but what they lack is a crisis communication plan. These set out exactly how to communicate with media and other stakeholders when things reach crisis point. It's situations like this that severely test your ability to face the media. Your media interview skills will be severely put to the test but there's more to crisis communication planning than training a competent spokesperson.

This chapter isn't intended to answer all of your questions on how to respond in a crisis. Likewise, it's not a manual for how to prepare for one. For that, you need to consult with a senior public relations professional, preferably one with a track record in crisis communication. But as a leader, you do need to know how responding to a crisis has changed in the digital age. It bears little resemblance to life before the advent of social media. You also need to know where you fit into the picture. This will depend on the size of your organisation and the priority you place on its reputation.

> # "It takes 20 years to build a reputation and five minutes to ruin it. If you think about that, you'll do things differently."
>
> 🗨 **Warren Buffett**

What is a crisis?

Before we focus on dealing with crisis communication, we need to determine exactly what a crisis is. The Oxford English Dictionary defines it as, "A time of intense difficulty or danger."

What's more interesting is the Chinese word for crisis. It's made up of two characters. These are 'danger' and 'opportunity.' This is significant because it suggests that while a crisis is dangerous in some way, there's also a possibility of something good emerging from it.

That may seem hard to believe but a crisis dealt with properly can benefit an organisation in the long run. Some companies around the world have grown their reputations following a crisis because they communicated compassionately, honestly and quickly.

Many more have failed miserably. They've been slow to respond, withheld information and not shown enough empathy for victims.

This is why a crisis communication plan is so vital. Without one, the delay in your response prevents you from responding as you must in today's world. That's because in these days of 24 hour news and social media, you have 15 minutes before your first statement must be issued.

That may seem like no time at all but it's a necessity. The story will probably show up on social media before you even know about it. Then people will start talking on social media, some will start speculating and others panicking. It'll spread like wildfire and within minutes it'll be picked up by traditional media.

During this period, which may only be a matter of minutes, everyone will wonder where you are. Are you in control? What are you doing to help? Do you even know what's happening? And most importantly, do you care? If you can't respond immediately, you'll damage your reputation.

That first call from traditional media will ask for comment on what's happening and what you're doing about it. Obviously, you'll know little but you must have something for the media. Otherwise the first news story will focus on speculation and emotion from social media chatter and all the story will say about you is, "Pete Burdon Ltd was unwilling to comment." That story will then be placed on news outlet websites and shared through multiple social media channels.

Holding statements

How are you supposed to respond in 15 minutes, particularly when there will be so many other things to do? The answer is to have holding statements prepared in advance for different scenarios. Then when the crisis hits, you fill in the gaps and send the relevant statement to your immediate stakeholders first, closely followed by the media. Here's an example of a holding statement that's ready for the death or serious injury of one or a number of staff members.

Statement from (Spokesperson) regarding (Say what incident is) at (YOUR) Organisation

We've just learnt of the situation and not all the relevant details are known at this stage. What I can confirm is that (explain what you can say, but don't speculate).

Our hearts go out to (whoever affected). We're doing all we can to support everyone who has been affected by this. For example (say something you are doing).

We're also working with relevant authorities to find out what happened (If applicable).

When facts are known, we'll be updating the website at www.peteburdonltd.com.

We'll hold a press conference at our premises at (time). All media are welcome. (If applicable)

Thank you

You need statements like this that cover the most likely and most serious crises you may face. They'll satisfy your stakeholders in the initial stages of the crisis before you have time to gather all the facts. Before you create these statements, you need a brainstorming session to see what scenarios you need statements for.

These could include:

- Death or serious injury of staff
- Fire
- Natural disaster
- Product recall
- Extortion attempt
- Sexual misconduct allegations
- Data breaches
- Employment disputes
- Protests

These will depend on the nature of your organisation. This list merely covers a few examples to get you thinking. Always remember that speed is of the essence with holding statements. That's why you need to do everything possible to have them ready to send at a moment's notice. Delays can be costly in terms of reputation and safety. Does your organisation have holding statements ready to go? If you don't have any, its money well spent to get them written. Again, this is where your leadership is vital. If you put crisis communication planning on the back burner, you'll pay the price if something happens. If you don't have a plan or public relations staff, you should contact a public relations company to help you put one together. The speed with which crisis communication has changed in the digital age means it's too late to call in help when a crisis erupts. Holding statements are a vital part of any plan.

Another thing that often delays their release is the clearance process. Some organisations insist on five or 10 people giving their permission before anything is sent to the media. In a crisis, this is a mistake. It causes fatal delays. The only way to fix this problem is to go through this clearance process well in advance. Once the statements are produced, send them through the clearance procedure. This must be done on the understanding that the person charged with filling in the gaps is able to make minimal changes.

> # "You can't fatten a pig on market day."
>
> 🗩 **John Howard,** former Australian Prime Minister

Media messages in a crisis

Just as you need a three point message in media interviews, you need the same thing for a crisis. These may change as the crisis progresses but they must be the focus of all communication. This includes media interviews and all other avenues you use to update relevant stakeholders. This doesn't mean you withhold facts. You should communicate all the facts that you can as you learn more. There'll be things you can't share but make sure this only happens when there's good reason to withhold something. We covered crisis media messages earlier. These came under the 3R system and it's important to have these prepared in advance along with your holding statements.

Who does what when the crisis erupts?

Depending on the nature of your crisis, the media attention and interest from other stakeholders can be overwhelming. There will be many jobs that need to be done. If these aren't assigned in advance, a calm and measured response is impossible. The size and nature of your organisation will determine who and how many people fill these roles. Many of them will be filled by public relations professionals if you have them on staff but if you're a sole trader, you may cover them all yourself. See below for a brief description of the major roles that are important in any crisis event.

Crisis Communication Leader

This person is in charge of the communication team during the crisis. He or she will need to sign off anything that's sent out to groups affected by the crisis. There's a distinction here between the Crisis Communication Leader and Operational Response Crisis Leader (ORCL). This latter role must also be filled by someone in your organisation. The Crisis Communication Leader manages the team but also spends time with the ORCL. This is the only way to keep up to date with what's happening and what new information should be shared with stakeholders.

Media Spokesperson

The rules about media spokespeople change slightly during a crisis. Normally, there should be a single spokesperson per issue which would usually be a CEO or board chairperson but with a crisis, that's not always realistic because media will approach all sorts of people for comment.

If they all refuse to say anything, it can look like they're hiding something. The answer is to share the media message with the entire staff. If asked a question, they can relay a key point from the media message, then defer to the overall spokesperson for any detail. There should always be an overall spokesperson who is the go-to person for any detail. If you're a large business and the crisis relates to some technical issue, the official spokesperson may need back-up help from a technical expert for media interviews or press conferences.

It's vital that staff who relay a key point don't get into any detail. If they do this without understanding the media interview process, they risk having their words taken out of context or being misquoted without even knowing it.

Media Liaison Officer

Every organisation needs someone to act as a direct link with the media. While the spokesperson does the media interviews, someone needs to liaise with the media. This includes jobs such as organising interviews and press conferences. The media liaison officer (MLO) should be the first port of call for journalists. He would coordinate with the spokesperson about potential interviews and should understand the requirements of journalists.

The most obvious example of this distinction between spokesperson and MLO is in the political arena. The prime minister or president is the party's key spokesperson, while a team of press secretaries (MLOs) organise interviews, create relationships with journalists and look for ways to generate positive media attention for their leader and the party.

Writer

The writer produces all the written material for the media and other groups. This includes holding statements, press releases, letters to parents and social media updates. This role is often taken by the MLO.

Digital Manager

Once the crisis is underway, the digital manager (DM) keeps the communication leader informed of what's happening in both traditional and social media. The DM must be in contact with the MLO so that rumours or misinformation can be corrected and trending questions can be answered in future updates. This person also adds new information to websites and social media platforms.

Telephone staff

Telephone staff are important in any crisis as they're often the first port of call for reporters and other stakeholders. Their role is to answer the most basic questions but otherwise to direct people to the latest information on the organisation's website. With media calls, they'll need to be careful not to be dragged into detailed conversations or interviews. A quick reference to a key point from the media message is all they should say, apart from well known facts. Media should then be directed to the MLO who will then coordinate with the official spokesperson.

PR Expert

If you experience a serious crisis, you'll need support from a public relations expert. If you don't have a public relations department or contract a public relations consultancy, you need to find someone who can help you when a crisis breaks. It'll be too late to start looking when it happens. Also remember that you need to start communicating immediately. Your public relations expert will be a great help but you can't delay your response until she's on the ground.

Who should fill these roles?

In a large organisation, those in the crisis communication team may play a single role while there could even be more than one person in some roles. If you have a large public relations department, most roles will be taken by staff from there but in a small business, there may only be two people available. It totally depends on the size and nature of your organisation.

As leader, you'll need to think carefully about what roles you'll play. You may be too busy playing your part in the operational response to worry about leading the communication effort. If you have a public relations department, someone there would obviously claim that job and if you contract a public relations company, a consultant from there may slot in nicely. If you do have these people, use them. They are experts in this area. Also remember that not all crises will be emergencies. Some will be reputational only, such as allegations of impropriety by staff members.

In most situations I've dealt with, the CEO is too busy to lead the communication team and has staff for that function. However, the leader does take responsibility for the spokesperson duties. In a serious crisis, it's important that the CEO is front and centre. It shows that the organisation is taking the situation seriously. The CEO is also usually the regular spokesperson and most qualified for the role. Public relations staff shouldn't be spokespeople. They can play every other role but reporters don't want to talk to them, they want to talk to the leader. You must take responsibility for this.

Create a list of core contacts

When the crisis hits, your organisation will need to communicate quickly with important stakeholders. To minimise the chances of your messages failing to get through, you need a triangular approach. In other words, have three ways to contact your most important groups because you can never guarantee a recipient will receive a single message. For example, spouses of your staff may arrive at work to see if their partners are safe after a fire. You may have sent a message to their email addresses telling them everyone was safe and you wanted to keep the roads clear for fire engines but if you'd sent them a text message and posted on social media pages as well, it's more likely they'd have stayed at home.

This is also important from a reputation standpoint. If stakeholders don't get your messages and hear about the crisis through media, they may start criticising you on social media. This is common and can be quite scathing when emotions take over. It can also lead to media interest and create exciting sound bites for reporters searching for sources.

Suggested groups to maintain contact with:

- *The Crisis Communications Team members*
- *Your Board of Governors, especially the chair*
- *Staff*
- *Staff spouses*
- *Regular clients*
- *Suppliers*
- *Emergency services*
- *Neighbours*
- *Counselling services for staff*
- *Lawyer*
- *Insurer*
- *Public relations consultant*
- *Local politicians*
- *Media*
- *Local community*

This is only an indication and you'll need to create your own list. Exactly how you communicate will depend on the scenario you face. For example, if a bus crash only involved two workers, you may only phone their spouses and use less direct channels for everyone else. The important thing is that you've got all the contact information you may need at your fingertips.

Create communication channels

All stakeholders will get their news about the event from different places. This will either be directly from you, from traditional media sources or from social media. It's important that you have your own channels set up to communicate so people don't rely on others for their information.

While traditional media will be helpful and you need to use it, journalists are interested in producing stories rather than communicating all the mundane facts. On the odd occasion, they may also get things wrong.

People posting news on social media sites may also have their facts wrong. This is why you need to have multiple channels where you inform and broadcast your own news. The days are gone when newspapers, radio and television are the only places where people get their news. The following sub-sections discuss what you need to have organised.

Phone numbers

It's vital to have the phone numbers and email addresses of your most important stakeholders so that they can be contacted at a moment's notice, including after hours.

Text messaging system

A text messaging system is also important. This is the most efficient and quickest way to notify people. It's also the channel that'll work best in natural disasters such as earthquakes. The system should be able to send messages to selected groups. For example, parents from a selected school classroom or workers from individual departments.

Email

Systems that can send text messages can often send emails also. This is important as it increases the chances of the message getting through in one form or another. In less critical crises, it may be appropriate to send emails alone, while in others, multiple options should be used. If you don't have a text messaging system, you'll need a detailed list of emails for all stakeholders.

Dark website

Your organisation should have a dark website. This is a site that's developed before a crisis but isn't visible. It's turned on when the crisis begins with lots of pre-loaded information. If your budget prevents you from following this option, at the very least, someone needs immediate access to upload statements to your organisation's home page. Your website or dark website will be the shop window for your organisation throughout the crisis. It's where you'll place all new information and where to direct all stakeholders for updates. Even email and text messages should link back to more detailed information on the website.

Social Media

Social media has become a vital element in crisis communication. It's the reason you must respond within 15 minutes. People will expect regular posts. This will include obvious stakeholders as well as others you may not know. You want everyone to hear what you're saying about the crisis and not hear it from someone else who may have an axe to grind about your management.

Secondly, it'll give people a chance to ask questions about what's going on. These days, concerned stakeholders demand this. The digital manager will keep in touch with comments and bring these to the attention of the communication leader which will also take the pressure off phone lines.

The other vital ingredient you need in your social media mix is a monitoring system. There are many options to do this. These will send you emails whenever the keywords you have selected show up online and let you know what people are saying about you and what information they're seeking.

It will also let you know if misinformation is being spread. Such a tool can ward off a crisis because many organisations find there were warning signs before the crisis erupted. Often these can be found on social media. For example, a restaurant could find a few comments from recent customers complaining about a rude waiter. If management saw these comments, the issue could be resolved before the complaints started mounting up but if management was unaware of them, the number of complaints could lead to interest from traditional media. It's important to nip this in the bud before it gets serious and social media monitoring helps you to do this.

Some of these systems are free, but the best ones have ongoing costs. An Internet search will reveal all of your options.

New South Wales Police give masterclass

During the Sydney Siege of 2014, New South Wales Police showed how valuable social media is in a crisis. This was when a lone gunman held 18 people hostage in a central Sydney café for 16 hours.

The consistent updating of the NSW Police social media sites, particularly Twitter, was highly effective. By my calculations, their first Twitter post warning people to keep away from the area was up within minutes.

Then important information was added whenever there was anything new to report. This included one sentence tweets and Facebook posts, links to more detail including press conference footage and re-tweets of important posts from other organisations. This is something any organisation should do in the midst of a crisis. While any crisis you face may not be as public as this one, it's vital that stakeholders are kept up to date.

With police themselves releasing so much information, there was less risk that the public or media would go elsewhere to get their information. In crisis situations where those directly involved don't communicate quickly and regularly, people naturally look elsewhere for more information. These are often less credible sources or others who can only speculate.

No margin for error for spokesperson

As the spokesperson in a crisis, your margin for error is non-existent. While all of the tasks mentioned above must be carried out, your role as spokesperson is vital. Firstly, if you're not available, reporters will run stories on your crisis without your input. You should be able to avoid interviews in the first hour or two if a holding statement has been sent out but you'll soon have to front up for media interviews or a press conference. If it's a serious issue, you can't continue to release statements without appearing. Firstly, television is a visual medium so the crew will want pictures of you talking. Secondly, if it's a crisis where there are victims, you need to put yourself in front of the camera to show your sincere empathy towards those affected.

> "Nobody cares how much *you know*, until *they know* how much *you care*."
>
> 💬 **Theodore Roosevelt**

This is an area where many leaders fail. They try to avoid the television cameras at all cost but it's vital to front up. People want to know that you care. You can say this in a statement but it doesn't mean anywhere near as much as it does if they see you. They need to see the whites of your eyes. It's fine to send a holding statement initially but you can't continue to rely on this if it's a major crisis.

Also remember that there's no obligation on the media to use your statement. They could still say you refused to appear. They could also say your statement is on their website without showing its contents.

The media have the power to make you come across as a leader in control of a difficult situation or a villain who has let his stakeholders down, which is why you need to front up whenever they want you to.

In a nutshell, the media can be your friend and help you or your enemy who can cause you trouble. Work with them. Give them what they want while also getting your message out.

There are countless examples of leaders worsening a crisis by making costly mistakes in their dealings with the media. BP's Tony Hayward is a recent example. He highlighted the importance of 'staying on message' when he spoke for his company after the disastrous Gulf of Mexico oil spill in 2010.

His most famous blunder was an off-the-cuff comment. When apologising publicly to locals during a media interview he said, "We're sorry for the massive disruption this has caused to their lives." He should have stopped there but he continued, "There's no-one who wants this thing over more than I do. I'd like my life back."

Those last five words appeared in the media throughout the world along with the assumption that Hayward was more concerned about himself than the people of the Gulf who had lost their livelihoods or family members. That's a perfect example of how high the stakes can get during a crisis.

This is an important lesson for any spokesperson expressing empathy after a crisis erupts. Empathy is a vital message to get across but make sure that empathy is focused on those directly impacted, not yourself. This is a common mistake. For example, if a worker is killed in a freak accident, a spokesperson may say, "We're devastated by this shocking accident." That may seem like a good point to make but even if you're devastated, the message has to be focused on the victim's family, not you. A better message point would be, "We're devastated for the victim's family after this shocking accident."

Hayward made other mistakes in his role as media spokesperson during the oil spill. In the early stages, he wasn't consistently available to the media which meant he wasn't able to control the flow of information and be the media's first port of call. This might be the last thing you feel like doing in a situation like this but it's better that you be the focus of media publicity than others because other sources may be unsympathetic or they may not have accurate information. When you're not available, the media have no choice but to speculate or use less credible sources to interview.

Another mistake Hayward made was to downplay the magnitude of the crisis in the early stages. In one media interview he said, "The environmental impact of this disaster is likely to be very, very modest."

If the impact is unknown, you shouldn't speculate or downplay the damage. Speculation can come back to haunt you if you're wrong. This happened to Hayward. You can also be accused of failing to take the crisis seriously if you downplay its impact.

Let's take another example to make this point. A school bus crashes on the way home from a camp. Two students are killed but it's the first time a student has ever been killed in that school's 100 year history.

A school principal could say, "This is an unfortunate incident but this school has a fantastic safety record with only two deaths in 100 years." While that may be true, the parents of the dead students won't think so. Others will also think the principal is dismissing the deaths as unfortunate but not of serious concern.

Fishermen in the Gulf of Mexico would have thought the same way when Hayward said the environmental impact of the spill was likely to be very modest.

What's changed in the digital age?

The digital age has transformed crisis communication planning. The way you must communicate in a crisis now bears little resemblance to what it was like before the 24-hour news cycle and social media. This has caught many organisations off guard because the success of your response will be measured by the speed at which you start communicating. Before the digital age, all you had to worry about was tonight's television news or tomorrow's newspaper which gave you plenty of time to prepare your media response.

There was also no immediate way for other stakeholders to start discussing the crisis or your response to it. They could only use the telephone or meet in person which also meant that the media couldn't eavesdrop on those conversations.

But now this has all been turned on its head. News stories are produced and placed online and through social media immediately. This happens with or without your input. Stakeholders also talk about the crisis within minutes of it erupting and they critique your response for all to see.

As the leader, you need to make sure your organisation is ready to respond to the media and other stakeholders in a crisis. Is there a crisis communication plan in place? If so, how effective would it be in today's world? These are questions you need to ask. As spokesperson, you also need to be ready for media interviews and press conferences. You must be confident in doing this. The only way to gain that confidence is through ongoing practice.

Along with this media interview practice, you need regular crisis communication drills. This is the only way you'll find out where the weaknesses are in your plan. This directive will need to come from you otherwise they will continually be postponed because something supposedly more important always comes up. If your reputation is valuable to you and your organisation, nothing is more important.

If you need help getting your crisis communication plan underway, see the resource section at the end of the book.

Where else are media skills handy?

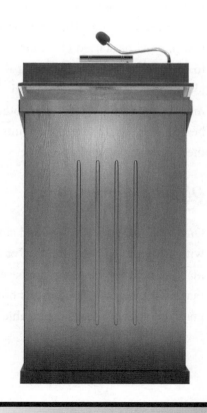

CHAPTER ELEVEN

Where else are media skills handy?

This book has focused primarily on giving you the skills to face the news media with confidence. That's also been the focus of my clients when attending my media training workshops. One piece of feedback I consistently get is that the skills aren't only applicable in media interviews but many other areas as well.

One skill that most people find difficult to master is breaking up what they want to say into a short and simple message. How many times have you seen someone take what seems like eternity to get to the point in a business meeting? By the time the speaker makes the point, you've lost interest or started checking your emails on your phone. The key is to know exactly what the point is before you make it. Then you need to break it down to its core and make it quickly. That's why a media message can be useful in many other business contexts. Most things can be broken down to three key points but if not, it's still important to break them down as much as possible.

Difficult conversations

One situation where a clear and simple message is vital is when dealing with difficult conversations. I've run workshops on this with senior management teams. These are based on media training principles. Since that's not what you bought this book for, I won't dwell on this but you may find a few of the transferrable skills useful.

The 3Rs system is as applicable during difficult conversations as it is during a media interview in the midst of a crisis. Let's take an example. You have an employee who wants to talk to you about getting a pay rise. He hasn't had one for three years and consistently gets great feedback from his immediate superior.

Your focus can be Regret, Response and Reassurance. When he asks you for the raise, you can use regret/empathy. "I can understand why you want a raise, particularly since you've clearly done such a wonderful job over the last three years."

That'll make the worker feel better. You may then tell him that the company is unable to give anyone a pay rise because of the tough economic times. Then you move to the response, "As soon as we're able to raise wages, you'll be the first on the list." You can then offer whatever else you can do for the worker.

Then you can move to reassurance, "I want you to know that we really value your work here."

You can see how the three point message can work in many different situations. Just as they do with media interviews, lots of people forget to use the regret/empathy point with difficult conversations. Often that's all people want to hear.

The other highly transferable skill is the ability to predict difficult questions. This can be done with the formula: Where, When, Why, What, Who and How?

Body language is also vital here. As we covered earlier, your body language and tone of voice accounts for 93 percent of the message that is received by the other person, when conversations relate to feelings and attitudes.

Presentations

Most spokespeople try to cover too many points in media interviews. The same is true of most executives when it comes to giving presentations. How many times have you seen someone give a PowerPoint presentation, rolling out point after point after point without an interesting analysis of any of them?

You may be one of them. When asked why they cover so many points, the common answer is that they're all important. They say it'd be impossible to leave any out.

The problem with this is that the audience won't remember any of them. They'll switch off after the first few because of boredom. In other words, the whole experience will have been a waste of time for everyone.

Just like a media interview, the answer is to select the three most important points and focus on those throughout. Time and space won't be at a premium as they are in media interviews but remember that audience members only have so much space available to store new information. They'll only remember a few points and that's only if they're presented in an interesting way.

This is why you should brainstorm to find these points, just like you do before a media interview. The process is almost identical. Your points need be ones you want to communicate but more importantly, they must be of interest to your audience.

You then need to find ways to back up those points. This is similar to creating sound bites in media interviews but the difference is that you'll have more time. This means you can use stories to back up your points which is the best way to make your points stick with audience members. We all find it difficult to remember fact after fact but if only a few facts are presented and backed up with interesting stories, we remember the point and act on it. That must be the aim of any presentation. It's pointless presenting information if people won't remember the points you are trying to make.

The only requirement when selecting stories is that they make the point you are trying to get across. People love stories and remember them and that's why they're the best way to get points to stick in the minds of your audience. You may think you don't have any relevant stories to back up your points but you tell stories every day and have had hundreds of experiences throughout your life that you can use as stories in your presentations.

For example, when I present to audiences on media training, the power of body language is always one of my points. I back up its importance by referring to the story I told earlier in this book about my disastrous interview when trying to secure a place in journalism school. That story takes an abstract concept and brings it to life. It also interests the audience because everyone likes stories. It helps me to keep their attention and I also know that they'll remember the point because they always remember the story. I've tested it.

You can also use statistics to back up points but don't use too many as this will only confuse people and become boring. Other sound bite elements can be effective in presentations, as long as they're reflecting one of the points you're trying to make. Comedy and examples are two that can work well if used in the right context.

You can see how similar this is to media interview preparation. If you're still unconvinced, there's nothing wrong with giving your audience a handout focused on all the other points you wanted to cover in the presentation. They can read that in their own time. That way there's more chance the material will sink in.

What's changed in the digital age?

The sheer volume of information people receive these days means it's never been more important to have the skills to break down what you want to say to its core. That's what a media message does. It's also what you need to do in many other areas of your work. The use of sound bite elements is now important in all areas of business.

While we use them to get our points through the editing process in media interviews, they're also effective in getting people to remember points in other environments. For example, a client told me how he used them in board meetings. Instead of making a point with mundane language that would probably be forgotten, he dressed his points up into sound bite language. You can do the same.

The other area where these skills become effective in the digital age is when producing your own videos. These are becoming more important as people move from text to video for their news and information. Remember that YouTube is now second only to Google in search engine popularity.

Your videos will need to focus on a clear message that cuts to the chase and your body language will also need to portray that same message, just as it must in a media interview.

These points all show that media skills are important in so many areas in the digital age. Even people who'll never face the news media will need them to be effective communicators.

CHAPTER TWELVE

How to attract positive media coverage

CHAPTER TWELVE

Attracting positive media coverage

So far, the focus of the book has been on dealing with the media when they approach you or in other words, how to react when the media want something. But this shouldn't be the only time you deal with the news media. There'll be many opportunities for you to be proactive and initiate contact. As I mentioned earlier, most encounters with the media can be seen as opportunities, not threats.

By knowing what interests a reporter and understanding how to approach them, you can generate positive publicity for yourself or your organisation. If you're a CEO and spokesperson, you may have a public relations department to do most of this for you or you may use the services of a public relations consultancy. Regardless, there's still a role for you to play here and for the work that may be the responsibility of others, it's still important that you understand the process involved. It'll help you understand the news media better and allow you to suggest potential story ideas to your public relations experts so that they can pitch them to the news media.

Take advantage of the opportunity

In the digital age, coverage in traditional media has become more important. It seems that everyone now has their own news networks through social media and other web applications. They can publish anything they want at any time of the day or night but the third party endorsement that news organisations offer is great for reputations.

People know the stories you feature in go through media gatekeepers before publication. The assumption is that you must be an expert if you're quoted in the media and this causes you to stand out from the crowd as an individual and as an organisation.

> ## "All publicity is good, except an obituary notice."
>
> ### 🗩 Brendan F Behan

There are other benefits of generating positive media coverage. It creates goodwill in the community. This is important when crisis strikes. If people already know you're a credible organisation, they won't dismiss you as quickly as they would if this is the first they've heard of you.

By taking this proactive approach with the media, you'll also develop relationships with reporters and they'll then give you fair coverage when that negative story does appear. But if you don't co-operate and never approach them in the good times, you can expect less sympathy when the stakes rise.

What's the first step?

Before looking at what stories you or your organisation can tell, you need to look at what media to approach. What media outlet does your target market follow? This is the first question to answer. It'll depend entirely on the nature of your business. For example, if your market is corporate executives, your focus would be business magazines and business reporters at daily newspapers. If you're a school principal, you may focus specifically on local media within the area from which you attract students. Media directories are a great place to find your target outlets.

It's important to find the details of the best person to contact at media outlets and deal directly with them. For example, if your focus is education, you'd deal with the education reporter at a daily newspaper. If it's a national magazine, the editor is usually the best contact. In my experience, this is far more effective than sending material to some general address at that media outlet. Often that never gets to the right person, particularly if you don't know who that person is.

That job can be delegated but the next step can't. That's meeting those reporters deemed the ones who are most relevant. This should be an informal chat, possibly over a coffee at their local café. The aim of this is to let them know who you are and find out more about them and their needs as a reporter. Don't try to pitch a story idea to them at this stage but find out how they like to be contacted and at what times.

This shows them you're a genuine person who's interested in their needs. The next time material appears in front of them from your organisation, they'll look at it in a new light. They'll give it the time of day. That's more than can be said for a huge number of story pitches that clog up reporters' inboxes on a daily basis.

What do reporters want in their stories?

It's important that you only contact reporters with story ideas that may interest them. If you waste their time with ideas they'd never consider, they may never take you seriously again. As a reporter, I received hundreds of story pitches that were nothing more than advertisements dressed up as news. These are usually sent by people who have no understanding of what constitutes news or they're so wound up in their organisation that they're convinced their idea has merit. Don't fall into this trap.

In my experience, news stories fall into five distinct categories. If your idea doesn't fall into one of these, the chances are that it's not news.

The first and best opportunities for you are story ideas related to topical issues. For example, if you're a real estate agent and national house sale figures are released, you have a great opportunity. You can comment on the national story by relating it to your specific patch. Then pitch the story to the media in your area. Then the story is not only topical, it's also local. The same goes for any other industry.

What about topical events. If an Olympic Games is about to start, a school could have its own mini Olympics where students dress up as their favourite athlete. Local media would love that. Once again, it's topical and local. The possibilities are endless when it comes to piggybacking off topical issues.

The next category includes things out of the ordinary. Why not create your own event with a twist. A bald man who owned a restaurant in the United States a few years ago had almost no one visit on Tuesday nights. He decided to offer free dining for bald people. This created masses of media attention and soon filled up his restaurant with both bald and non-bald diners. What could you do?

Anything that's new or a first can be of interest. You won't receive media attention for every award you receive but the most notable or different may get coverage. Have you developed a new product that saves lives? If you have a new product or service that solves a particular problem, it could generate media interest. Don't forget niche media. If a new product only benefits a particular group, media focused on that group could be the better target. This isn't only because they'd be interested but because their readers may purchase the product.

The next category is human interest. This could be the worker who's leaving you after 50 years of service or someone who's succeeded against the odds. These stories focus specifically on people.

You won't be surprised to know that conflict sells. This might not be something you want to focus on but there could be a time for it. For example, if you're an employer, you could find a new government policy increases your compliance costs to the point where you need to make someone redundant. If this angers you and you could benefit from the publicity, you could approach media with your concerns. Always be careful with conflict. Make sure the subsequent publicity can't be turned against you.

Keep these categories in mind when looking for story ideas to pitch to reporters.

How do you contact the media?

With all media, you contact them by either telephone or email. Most prefer email in the first instance and this is something you should discuss with the reporters you meet. Don't make the mistake of using social media for this purpose. While reporters do use social media as a source of news and they post regularly, most don't want to be pitched to this way.

When pitching by email, the most important part is the subject line. This is the first thing the reporter will see. If it doesn't grab their attention immediately, it'll be deleted without a second thought. This should come straight to the point, be as brief as possible and interesting enough to encourage the reporter to open the email. They get hundreds of emails a day and don't have time to open them all. If your subject line says something like, 'Press Release' or 'Announcement' then your message won't see the light of day.

The body of your message should sum up your story idea in two or three sentences. You should also say why you think it would interest their audience. That's the one criteria they'll use in deciding whether your idea is worth pursuing. An attractive quote is also a good idea.

Pitches these days should usually be tailored specifically for the reporter you're targeting. Before the digital age, the same pitch was often sent to multiple reporters. This didn't take their target market into account, the type of media outlet they represented or even the particular focus of individual reporters. These days you target individuals. If a reporter works for a local newspaper, she'll only be interested in stories that affect the local area. In contrast, a national newspaper will focus on Australia or New Zealand as a whole.

Let's take that real estate example. If you had house sales figures for Australia, a reporter for a national newspaper would be interested in what trends had taken place throughout the entire country but if you wanted to get coverage in a Sydney newspaper, the focus of your pitch would be the Sydney figures and how they related to the rest of the country. If you could break the figures down further, you'd attract interest from community newspapers.

It's also a good idea to look at a reporter's recent stories and comment on those in your pitch. For example, "I see you've focused recently on the impact of the new rate increases. As a small business, we have also been badly affected."

Of course, there'll be exceptions to this targeting process. If you're a prime minister, mayor or you have breaking news that will interest a huge list of media outlets, you may contact them all at once. In that case, you may also issue a press release.

When is a press release necessary?

One question I often get asked is, "Do I need to send a press release with my pitch?" A press release is similar to a news story you see in your newspaper. The difference is that you write it and send it to media. The idea is that they use some of the information in it to produce their own news story.

There's been much debate in media and public relations circles over the last few years about the need for press releases. Some say the press release is dead, while other say it's very much alive.

My view is that it depends on where you plan to send it and what staff you have. As already discussed, if you have major news that'll interest media across the spectrum, a press release is a good idea. This is common with politicians, associations and other national bodies.

When you have news that editors won't hold the front page for, the need for a press release depends on the news organisation you're targeting. For major daily newspapers, reporters are unlikely to use information directly from your press release. They normally decide whether your pitch is worthy of a story and if it is, they'll ring you for an interview.

There are exceptions to this rule. If you have public relations staff and the story isn't time sensitive, a press release is worth the effort. The same goes for non-time sensitive stories that are important to you. This could be a new book you've written, a good cause you're trying to promote or a number of other possibilities. But if it's a topical issue you want to comment on, or something you'd like coverage for but isn't vital, a pitch will do.

Some people will tell you that a press release is needed for anything but this view hasn't been echoed by reporters from daily newspapers whom I've spoken to. Some want them but many don't. Another important reason I suggest you don't always go to the trouble of writing a press release unless you have public relations staff is because you won't get around to it or won't have time.

Sending an email pitch is less time consuming and simpler. This is something you'll do. As I've said, the result is often the same and you should take advantage of any opportunity for publicity.

Local newspapers are different. These often have a single reporter working on them, so they welcome any help they can get. Their deadlines are also weekly or bi-weekly, rather than hourly or daily. That means there's less pressure to contact them immediately. They may even cut and paste your press release into the newspaper without editing it.

The same goes for trade publications. They often have a lone person working on them and there's also more space for their stories than in metropolitan daily papers. That means press releases can be effective.

Radio and television are different again. The press release is less necessary if it's a news bulletin you're aiming for. Their stories last a matter of seconds, so they want minimal detail. Also, as audio and visual mediums, they'll definitely want an interview. Radio reporters need your voice and television news programmes need you in person. If you're approaching a more detailed news programme or current affairs show, a press release is well worth the effort. Obviously, both broadcasting mediums will still need a convincing pitch before they consider your idea.

These are general comments. Every reporter is different and each has their own preferences. You need to find out what your target reporters want.

Angles

You'll see by reading newspapers that each story has a particular focus, or in media terms, an angle. These are important to find because it is the angle, rather than the topic itself, that forms the basis of stories. You need to follow this same principle in your pitches or press releases.

Let's say a local business is about to close. The topic would be, "Business to close," but that'd never be the angle of the story. An angle on that topic would be something like, "40 workers to be made redundant." So when we talk about stories, we are also talking about angles or a particular focus on a topic. Always remember to narrow down your pitch from a topic to an interesting angle.

How to write a press release

If you do decide that a press release is a good idea, it's important that you write it professionally. Otherwise reporters won't give it the attention it deserves. The following details cover the process.

Firstly, the most important parts are the headline and the lead.

The headline

This must grab the attention of the receiver, just as a headline does in a newspaper. Headlines are best kept to one line but two can be used if necessary. That's because you only have a few seconds to convince the journalist to read on. A look through the front page of your local metropolitan or national newspaper will give you examples of great headlines.

The lead

This is industry lingo for the first paragraph. Just as the headline needs to get the reader interested enough to read on, the lead must do the same. As many of the questions, where, when, why, what, who and how must be covered in the first paragraph. It shouldn't be longer than 25 words.

Writing style

Releases should all be written in third person. This means they shouldn't be written as if you are writing it, but a third party. That means the words 'I' or 'we' must never be used in a headline or lead. This is different from a holding statement, such as in the example shown earlier.

The body

The body is the remainder of the release. It should build on the lead and get straight to the point. It should only include information that is necessary to explain the story. It builds on the angle and doesn't include all the little details.

Direct quotes

Direct quotes are the exception to the rule about not using first person. They are all in first person. Quotes use the subject's language word for word, or verbatim. You'll usually be the subject, so you can create the quotes yourself. These are a vital part of the release because they bring it to life. Use the sound bite elements described earlier in the book to write your quotes. There's no rule about how many quotes to include but always have at least two, including one as the second or third paragraph. The quotation marks signify the quote.

Boiler Plate

This is the last paragraph where you briefly describe what your organisation does. This is only necessary if this hasn't been covered earlier on. It should be one sentence or two at the most.

Contact information

All releases must include contact information for the media who want to get hold of you. This is often overlooked. Two phone numbers is a good idea, while an email address can also be added. Without contact information, there's little likelihood that your story will be covered by anyone. Not only will they be unable to find you, you'll also lack credibility.

Numbers

Numbers below 10 should be written, while the actual number can be used for 10 and above. For example, eight, nine, 10, 11. This is standard journalistic style.

Proofread

Once the release is complete, always get someone to proofread it. You should already have done a spell check. The proofreading is to give it a final clearance for grammar and any other mistakes. It's also important that journalists and their audiences will be able to understand it. We all have jobs and interests that we know about in detail. Sometimes we wrongly assume that lots of that knowledge is known by everyone. That's why it's important for someone outside your industry to look over the release with an objective eye. If they can't understand it, chances are the media won't either and your release will be destined for the rubbish bin.

Small words

Use small words whenever possible. Releases need to be as clear and concise as possible. There are no points for big words, only less chance of publication.

Keep brief

Keep releases as brief as possible. Many journalists won't even look at a second page. If you find this difficult, remember press releases are a carrot to get the media interested, not a document covering a subject in its entirety.

To see how these elements come together in a press release, including the structure of direct quotes, see the following example.

Acme Limited ← ORGANISATION NAME

Media Release
July 10, 2012 ← DOCUMENT DESCRIPTION & DATE

Rate increase sees local business cut staff | HEADLINE

This week's rate increase by Black City Council has led to the loss of 10 jobs at a well known local business. | LEAD

Acme Limited COE, Joe Blogs, said the successive rate increases had put major pressure on the business but this last one left them with no choice but to proceed with redundancies.

"In tough economic times it's hard enough for businesses to stay afloat but with the added pressure of rate increases, it's a bridge too far for us" says Mr Blogs. | DIRECT QUOTE

"How does the council expect the region's growth rate to rise when they make it impossible for businesses to function properly?"

Mr Blogs said he hoped to retain his other 50 employees but this would be dependent on economic conditions and the possibility of more rate increases.

Acme Limited is a furniture manufacturer in Black City. It is one of the region's biggest exporters, with more than 60 percent of its products going to offshore buyers.

"BOILER-PLATE"

ENDS

SIGN-OFF

For more information:
Joe Blogs:
Phone 03 444 5555 Mobile 0271 890 888
Email joe.bloggs@acmeltd.nz
www.acmeltd.com

CONTACT DETAILS

Points to remember when pitching stories

Never argue with a reporter or editor if they decide not to accept your pitch. It's their decision. You may think it's the best story idea since sliced bread but they may have a totally different viewpoint. There are many reasons story pitches are turned down. For example, you may not have found the most interesting angle or there could be lots of news to compete with on the day you pitched the idea. Another common reason can be that a similar story was produced recently which is another reason why it's a good idea to see what the reporter has covered lately.

As I mentioned earlier, the job of pitching stories may be the responsibility of someone else in your organisation but you'll still be the spokesperson. This means you need to be available when the media ring. You can still buy some time but never more than 15 or 30 minutes. If you're in meetings all day, it's not the best time to be pitching a story to the media. This is particularly so if the story isn't time sensitive.

Become the media source for your niche

The best way to get regular and positive media coverage is to become a known source for media comment in your industry. Commenting on topical issues is by far the best way to get coverage. You already know the media are interested in the topic and this also gives you a great opportunity to cement yourself as a thought leader in your niche.

To do this, you or your public relations team need to be on alert at all times. As soon as an issue relevant to your industry breaks, someone needs to produce a media pitch with your views on that issue. It may be how it affects your particular area, your condemnation of it or another interesting angle. The more you do this, the more coverage you'll get.

Your success at this will depend on your speed of response. For example, let's say research is released showing that unemployment among the over 50s has jumped to record levels and your business is focused on finding work for this group. If you see the research, you should quickly create a pitch and send it off immediately. If you wait to write a press release and get others to edit it, you'll be too late. This will obviously depend on where you decide to send your pitch. If it's a monthly trade publication, you can relax but if it's The Sydney Morning Herald or the New Zealand Herald, you must send something immediately. The reporters may already be writing their story.

There are places you can go to register yourself as a source for reporters when they need expertise in your area. One of these is HARO.com, while another is Sourcebottle.com. By all means, sign up to these but you'll be far more successful if you get proactive and approach reporters yourself.

The best idea is to create your own media database of relevant reporters and focus on that small group. Once you've been proactive for a while, the media will start approaching you.

Bear in mind that this'll be dependent on your media interview skills. If you can't give interesting quotes and sound bites when you talk to reporters, they won't come back and if your body language is poor, you won't be asked back to a television studio for your expertise. That's why it's vital to develop and maintain the media interview skills covered in this book.

Don't forget guest columns

A guest column is an article written by someone as a one-off for a magazine or newspaper. The big difference here is that you write the article rather than the journalist and you're identified as the author. Some leaders have public relations staff write the columns for them.

They're always written in first person and take many forms. Sometimes people with specific knowledge are asked to write columns on particular issues. For example, after a sudden increase in the price of oil, a magazine may ask an expert in the petrol market to write a column on the chance of more increases.

Your local or metropolitan newspaper may be interested in a column from you. Remember the example earlier about the person who found jobs for the over 50s. That person would have had a great chance of finding space for guest columns on the issue.

All columns have one thing in common. They're of interest to the readership of the publication they're written for. They're also a great way for the authors to grow the credibility of themselves and their organisations.

What information could you have that would make an interesting column? Once again, topical issues tailored to the audience of your target publications are your best chance. This is a fantastic way to grow your reputation.

Look through your target publications to see what sorts of columns are included. This'll give you some great ideas.

What's changed in the digital age?

A lot has changed when it comes to generating positive media attention in the digital age but one thing hasn't. Reporters still prefer to receive your pitches through email or telephone but some people make the mistake of doing this through social media.

Having said that, social media has its place. Reporters do use social media to look for newsworthy information so by all means, place your views and stories all over the web, just don't make it your primary way of contacting the media. It's also a great way to get your stories out to your market without the need for a media middleman but don't forget that most people still get their news from official channels, even if some may reach these channels through social media platforms.

When you do find yourself in media stories, social media is a great way to get these in front of the people you want to see them. Before the digital age, you had to hope people bought the newspaper or watched the television news bulletin that you were featured in. Now you can send links to all this information through your social media networks and websites.

When it comes to pitching to the media, another significant development has created another option. You've always been able to send written pitches and press releases but now video is growing in popularity. With the development of the multimedia journalist, news organisations are starting to want written material and video. You'll have noticed that major newspapers usually have a video to accompany their stories online. This will give them the option of including you in the video and it creates another opportunity for you to generate positive publicity.

Television networks may still want to interview you themselves but if you send a video as part of your pitch, they can see if you'd be a suitable commentator. They often use well known experts for their programmes because they know what they're getting so if you send them a quick 60 second video with a few relevant and interesting comments, they're more likely to invite you as an expert onto their news bulletins or extended programmes. If you have public relations people organising your pitches, this is one task you can't delegate. Good body language and the use of interesting sound bites are what television reporters and producers will be looking for in these videos. Just follow the advice earlier in the book to master this art.

What if you're misquoted?

CHAPTER THIRTEEN

What if you're misquoted?

As I've already stressed, the best way to avoid being misquoted or your words being taken out of context is to follow the advice in this book. That doesn't mean it won't ever happen to you but it'll significantly reduce the chance.

Remember, reporters aren't perfect and make their own mistakes from time to time and it's important to understand that this is almost never done on purpose. I was guilty of this myself once while I was covering a court case.

I committed what some would call the cardinal sin of court reporting. I used the wrong person's name when writing about a man who was sentenced for possession of cannabis. More on what happened in that scenario shortly.

You'll always hear stories about reporters who make up quotes or continually get stories wrong. These are so rare that they're not worth worrying about but you do need to know what to do if something does go wrong.

If you think you've been misquoted, the first thing to do is take a deep breath and have another look at the story. You'll always be your own worst critic, so what may appear to be a disaster may not seem so bad at second glance. If you're still unhappy, show the story to colleagues and friends. What do they think? When I worked as a media advisor, I often had calls from clients concerned about how they were portrayed in a story. Most of the time I thought reporters had written pretty balanced and fair stories. It's important to remember here that the reporters aren't working for you which means that their focus won't be to make you shine. Don't expect them to produce something that your own public relations department would be proud of.

The next step, if you're still dissatisfied, is to make sure you were misquoted. In other words, did you say the words you were quoted as saying? This may seem obvious but many people complain even though they were accurately quoted. This is usually where they claim to have been taken out of context. This is a difficult one. Clearly, there are times when spokespeople are taken out of context and it changes the meaning of what they were trying to say but remember that a reporter will never use everything you say in edited stories which means that everything used is taken out of context to some extent.

In the example I used earlier, BP boss Tony Hayward could have complained that his statement was taken out of context when he was quoted as saying, "I want my life back." Those five words were used during a conversation about the devastation caused by the oil spill and what BP was doing to mitigate the damage. While he could claim that it was taken out of context, he still said those words.

The next step is to determine how much damage the story could cause to your reputation or that of your organisation. If it's relatively minor, you may be best to let it go. If you do choose this option, it can still be a good idea to contact the reporter about it and say that you accept it was a genuine mistake but you'd like a note attached to that story when it's archived. That's because reporters often go back to old stories when producing new ones on a similar topic. If a note is attached to the story correcting the mistake, it won't be repeated in the future when a reporter researches background information on the topic.

If you're still unhappy, now's the time to contact the reporter or whoever produced the story. At this stage it's important to know exactly what your concern is. For example, if you think there are multiple errors, it may be best to focus on the one or two that you're most concerned about. If you believe your statement was taken out of context, make sure you have your argument ready.

The reporter may or may not take your complaint seriously. Regardless, it's courteous to contact her at this point. This is the time you need to know what you want done about the mistake. This is something to discuss with your colleagues or a public relations expert. If it's serious, a correction in the next newspaper, radio bulletin or television news programme is a possibility and you'll want the correction to be given prominence.

This is where the reporter's boss will need to be involved, whether that is an editor, executive producer or other title. If the reporter is uncooperative, you'll need to contact the person yourself. Otherwise the reporter may introduce you to the boss.

In my example, the man I identified as having been sentenced for possession of cannabis went straight to the editor. He could have come through me but this was an obvious mistake on my part and he had no obligation to be courteous. A correction went in the following day's newspaper on the front page and the headline had a red background, something that I'd never seen before. Clearly the editor saw the obvious mistake and acted quickly. This would have mitigated the circumstances if the man ever took legal action.

This story has an interesting end. The following week, the man I had wrongly identified was in court and convicted for the exact offence I had said he committed seven days earlier. That ended any chance of him taking legal action. He could no longer claim defamation.

Another option for a less serious mistake in a newspaper is to request a letter to the editor. It'd let you put your case with little editing. You'll need to keep it brief, usually less than 200 words. While anyone can write such letters, a cooperative editor would give yours priority. As a media advisor in government, this was something I did regularly. Interestingly, it was usually not after a news story but an editorial where the writer was harsh on ministers and even once, the prime minister.

There's another way to satisfy both parties when the mistake isn't fatal. There've been instances where the complainant and the editor agree to a type of compromise where the newspaper writes a positive story about the complainant or his organisation. That replaces the need for a correction. The idea is that positive publicity is always good for business and this allows the complainant to restore any reputational damage.

> ## "Publicity is absolutely critical. A good PR story is infinitely more effective than a front page ad."
>
> ### 💬 Richard Branson

There are other options but those discussed are the most common. With all of them, remember that there's a downside. If it's a negative issue you're dealing with, taking action will keep the story alive at least for a few more days. If you let it lie, reporters will move on to other stories and people will soon forget. This happened to a client of mine a few years ago. An opinion piece in a major business newspaper was weighted heavily against him and I contacted the newspaper for the client. They agreed to print a letter to the editor but said they still maintained the right to respond to that. We decided against the letter.

So what if the reporter's boss refuses to cooperate in any way and you are still unhappy?

Democratic countries throughout the world have their own institutions in place where citizens can complain about unfair media coverage. The most common for print and online media are press councils. These are self-regulatory bodies that work as independent forums to resolve complaints laid against print media organisations and their associated digital outlets.

The Australian Press Council can be found at www.presscouncil.org.au, while its New Zealand counterpart is at www.presscouncil.org.nz.

It's important to examine the powers of these organisations or the ones operating in your country as they normally have the power to ask media organisations to issue retractions and apologies. The councils also require the offending organisations to publish their adjudications. Make sure you analyse the website of your press council before making a complaint because policies vary. For example, if you make a complaint to the New Zealand Press Council, you must waive your rights to legal action following the council's decision. This is not required in Australia.

Democratic countries also have bodies to lay complaints against broadcasters. In Australia this is the Australian Communications and Media Authority. This can be found at www.acma.gov.au, while New Zealand's alternative is the Broadcasting Standards Authority or www.bsa.govt.nz. Both organisations, and others around the world, have specific powers to enforce on broadcasters who breach their country's codes of practice.

This can be a lengthy process. However, remember the first step is always to decide whether it's worth doing anything at all. If it is, the offending media organisation is next on the list. The chances are that you'll be satisfied with their response and that'll be the end of the matter but stick to the advice in this book and it's unlikely you'll ever be in this position.

Obviously legal action is always an option, but only in extreme cases.

What's changed in the digital age?

One major advantage in the digital age is the ease with which we can contact stakeholders through our own channels. As discussed in the chapter on crisis communication, you should have multiple ways of contacting people with an interest in your organisation. If you are badly misquoted, you should contact all relevant people through your own media to explain the mistake. That would have been far more difficult before the advent of the internet.

That should not stop you from dealing directly with offending media but it'll help set the record straight.

Another point worth mentioning to the offending organisation is how a correction or retraction would only grow its reputation. In today's world with citizen journalists, bloggers and billions of people using social media, many consumers of news wonder who to trust. If the offender admits the mistake, it shows that the organisation cares about accuracy and can be trusted as a genuine and honest source of news. These are the outlets people want to get their news from. So, if approached that way, admitting a mistake can be an opportunity for them, not an embarrassment.

"People care far more about how we respond to a mistake than the fact we made it in the first place."

🗩 **Pete Burdon, 2015.**

Where to from here?

CHAPTER FOURTEEN

Where to from here?

As a modern leader, you'll be able to delegate some of your media relations tasks. You may decide to hire a public relations consultancy to handle your ongoing work in this area. They would be your media liaison people, while they'd also be on hand if you ever found yourself in a crisis. They can also fulfil other roles that are outside the scope of this book. The other option you have is to employ one or more people in-house. This will depend on the size of your organisation and your budget.

This book will have given you a good intellectual understanding of media relations. It's important that you understand the principles of crisis communication planning and how to attract positive media coverage. Your leadership skills and attitude towards crisis communication are vital during crisis preparation and on the day but you don't need to be an expert in the finer details of this on a day-to-day basis. The same goes for generating positive media attention. That can be handled by public relations professionals.

However, there is one area you can't delegate to anyone else. I'm sure you recognise this, otherwise you wouldn't be reading this book. That's the role of spokesperson. You're the boss, so the buck stops with you.

When it comes to the spokesperson duties, you need both an intellectual understanding and a practical one which is why you need to go further than reading this book. You need to master the practical side of the media interview process.

It's no different from learning to ride a bike. First you learn what to do (this book), then you need to put that theory into practice and the best way to do that is by enrolling in a media training workshop. I can't emphasise the need for this enough. You may think you have the skills now but all you have is an understanding of what you must do. Putting it into practice is a different skill entirely.

So what should you look for in a media training workshop?

It's important to ask the following 10 questions when looking for a suitable trainer.

How practical is the training?

Because mastering media interviews is a practical skill, it's important that you have your share of time in front of a camera. For a full-day media training course, I recommend you be on camera at least five times. It's vital that you're asked to put what you have just learnt into practice.

What is the structure of the training?

Find out how the typical training day works. We've already covered the importance of being on camera but also make sure that the training is highly interactive and entertaining, rather than just a PowerPoint presentation and don't forget to make sure body language is covered.

Is the training customised?

Make sure the training will be tailored specifically to fit your requirements. This means using scenarios relevant to your business and training for your level of experience in front of a camera. It also means that you should have the ability to focus on specific aspects of media training if you wish.

What post-training education do they offer?

Despite what some say, you can't become an expert in one day. You can learn a great deal but not enough to be an instant expert. What does the firm offer past the training day? Refresher courses are important. Online training is also effective to complement the workshop.

Does the trainer have journalism experience?

It's important that the trainer understands the mindset of a journalist and this comes from working in the industry. It doesn't matter whether it's print, radio or TV but some experience asking the tough questions and living by deadlines is valuable.

Has the trainer worked on the other side of the camera?

Remember that journalists are only interested in a good story but as a spokesperson, your reputation is on the line. That's why someone who has worked in a full time capacity as a communications advocate for a high profile figure is important. Even someone who's had occasional spokesperson duties in high stakes situations is beneficial. It's important to know how a journalist ticks and ask the tough questions but it's just as important to have felt the fear as a spokesperson and know how to answer those tough questions, rather than just how to ask them.

Does the company look professional?

This is a basic requirement these days. If the company you're considering doesn't have a professional website, you should be concerned. That's not to say there aren't great trainers with bad websites but it's another point to take into consideration when making your choice.

Do they write a blog or other material to demonstrate their expertise?

Search their websites for regular blogs or articles they've written for the media. These can tell you a great deal about their expertise and they can also offer helpful advice.

Is the trainer a published author?

This will clearly demonstrate their expertise. It's not essential but it will give you added confidence that the trainer is proficient and is an expert in the field.

Are there high quality references available?

References should be available on the company website. If not, make sure you request some before making your decision. It can also be a good idea to talk to people who've been through the training. The company should be able to organise this for you.

You may or may not be able to find someone who ticks all of these boxes but it's a good gauge to decide who to use. You'll find there's a huge range in fees. However, it'd be a mistake to make your decision on price alone. Remember that anyone can call themselves a media trainer. Make sure you use the person you believe can add the greatest value to your media interview skills. It's important for you to master this. Don't forget that the best leaders are always the best communicators. Think of the leaders you most respect. I bet they're great in front of a television camera.

What's changed in the digital age?

In many ways, media training has changed little over the past 30 years but there are some subtle things you must be aware of in today's world that weren't necessary before the digital age arrived. These have been covered in the last section of each chapter. Make sure that any media trainer you choose understands these differences.

Online media training is also becoming more popular. If you do consider an online option, make sure it includes practical interviews where you put the theory to the test (See Resource Section). Otherwise you will gain an intellectual understanding, not the practical skills.

Five step process

When you have both a practical and theoretical understanding of media interviews, you can follow my five step process whenever you have an interview approaching. You'll recognise these steps as they sum up the first part of the book in a nutshell.

STEP ONE

Buy some time to prepare and ask the reporter questions to find out as much as you can about the intended focus of the interview. Remember not to buy too much time. This is also the time to weigh up whether you should agree to the request. In most situations, this is a good idea.

STEP TWO

Create your media message. This may be a simple task, or it could be more challenging. If it's a negative issue with a victim, start with the 3R system as a starting point. If you do find this step difficult, gather a colleague or two together for a brainstorm. This will usually uncover the best message fairly quickly.

STEP THREE

Give some thought as to what tough questions you may be asked. The best way to do this is to go through all the possibilities you can think of that begin with, Where? When? Why? What? Who? and How? For the most challenging, organise brief answers so you're ready for them.

STEP FOUR

Create sound bites for each of your three message points. Three is usually a good number of each one, but more should be added if it's a feature piece for a newspaper. The same applies for an extended news programme. Write out your sound bites on a single piece of paper beneath the message point they relate to. Have this sheet of paper in front of you for phone interview and study it well before television appearances or one-on-one interviews with reporters.

STEP FIVE

Practice, practice, practice. This is the most important step in the process. If you have limited time, at the very least get a colleague to ask you a few question and record it on her smart phone. Make sure you watch it back. This is the only way to see how well you did. If you have time, repeat this until you're satisfied.

THE LAST WORD

Now that you've read this book, you'll have a good understanding about what it takes to face the news media with confidence in today's world. It's a great first step but the second step is most important.

It's incredibly common for leaders to relax once they have got to this point in the process. They understand how to conduct a media interview and the importance of crisis communication planning. They also recognise the importance of practical media training and supporting their public relations team but they don't give it the priority it deserves. Sir Richard Branson sums this up well.

> "I suspect in most companies, the public relations person is down at No. 20 in the pecking order but here, he is fighting incredibly important battles. If a negative story starts running away with itself in the press and is not dealt with fast, it can badly damage the brand and so we put enormous weight on our PR people."

Can you relate to this statement? Are you prepared for that negative story or crisis? It's easy to put this on the back burner because it never seems urgent. A crisis doesn't erupt and reporters aren't breaking down the door to interview you so it doesn't seem necessary. But then suddenly a crisis or serious issue erupts, all hell breaks loose and you're thrust onto the media stage whether you like it or not. Just look at the news. It happens all the time. It's not always something as serious as an oil spill, but it's often something that threatens the very existence of an organisation. Businesses are usually unprepared and pay a heavy price. Don't let it happen to you. Take action now.

If you need help getting underway, have a look at the resource section of the book. There are some options there that can help you get started.

Pete Burdon

ABOUT THE AUTHOR

Pete Burdon

Pete is an accomplished author, experienced journalist, savvy communications specialist and a highly sought after media trainer.

He's trained countless corporate executives and entrepreneurs as well as leaders in a wide range of fields. These include local and national government, law, sport, medicine, school management and governance, tourism and aged care.

Pete understands what it takes to excel as a media spokesperson because of his experience on both sides of the microphone. He began his career as a reporter for a daily newspaper. Later, he moved into media management as a government press secretary. From there, he became a communication manager before starting his own media training business.

Pete is highly qualified for his role. He holds a Master of Arts Degree in Journalism from the University of Canterbury and a Master of Arts Degree in Communication Management from the University of Technology in Sydney.

Pete enjoys staying active and ran his first marathon at the age of 38. In his down time he enjoys a round of golf and socialising with friends. Pete's based in Christchurch, New Zealand where he lives with his wife Stephanie and daughter Olivia. He travels extensively to conduct workshops and give presentations at conferences and other events.

Want A Dynamic Speaker And Trainer At Your Next Conference?

Do your spokespeople know how to master media interviews in the digital age? Are you ready to communicate with journalists within minutes when a crisis strikes? Do your staff know what to do when approached by the media? When understood and mastered by everyone, knowledge in these areas goes a long way to cement reputations that are increasingly vulnerable in today's world.

PRESENTATION FORMATS

< Keynote

This engaging and thought-provoking programme will leave your conference or meeting participants with a new appreciation of the role of the news media, its requirements and how to create a mutually beneficial relationship with it.

Please allow 1 – 2 hours

< Full or Half Day Workshops

This is a 4 to 8 hour programme tailored to your individual organisation. This can focus entirely on the media interview process, crisis communication planning or a combination of these equally important areas. Includes workbooks and a crisis communication plan template for participants to take away.

< Two Day Workshops

These allow both the media interview process and crisis communication planning to be covered extensively. Includes workbooks and a crisis communication plan template for participants to take away.

www.PeteBurdon.com

Extraordinary Products To Grow Those Media Skills And Get Your Crisis Communication Plan Underway

Bolstering those vital media skills can now be done in the comfort of your own living room. Explore our range of programmes focused on media interview training, crisis communication planning and other useful information. Cement your reputation now and give yourself the peace of mind by knowing you're ready for any media encounter, positive or negative.

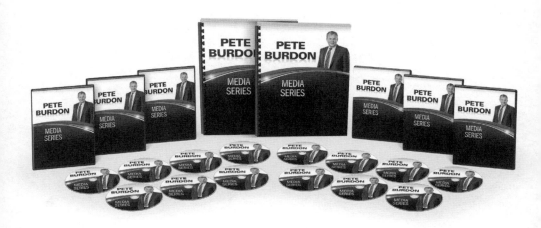

Visit my website to view the full range of products

www.PeteBurdon.com